DUBLIN 4

MAEVE BINCHY DUBLIN 4

POOLBEG

First published 1982 by
Ward River Press Ltd, Dublin

New edition published 1986
Reprinted 1990, 1992, 1994, 1996, 1997 (twice)

This edition published 1993 by
Poolbeg Press Ltd,
Knocksedan House,
Swords, Co Dublin, Ireland

A catalogue record for this book is available from the British Library.

ISBN 1 85371 102 0

Cover design by Pomphrey Associates
Printed and bound in Great Britain by
Cox & Wyman Ltd, Reading, Berkshire

Contents

For Gordon

with all my love

DINNER IN DONNYBROOK

1

She drew the dinner table six times and it always came out the same. If you put the host at one end and the hostess at the other it didn't work out. She would sit with her back to the window and have a man on either side of her. Fine so far. Dermot would sit opposite her with a woman on either side of him. Fine again, but what about the two places in between? Whatever way you did it you would have to have man sitting beside man, and woman beside woman.

She shook her head, puzzled. It was like those problems they had always done at school; if you have three missionaries and three cannibals on an island and the boat can only hold two . . . Not that it mattered of course, and anybody who knew how much time she had spent working it out would say she should spend a week in St Patrick's, but still it was very irritating. There must be a way.

'There is,' said her daughter Anna. She had telephoned Anna to talk about something else but brought the conversation around to the perplexing dinner table. 'At a party for eight, host and hostess can't sit opposite each other. You sit opposite the most important lady . . . and put Dad on that lady's left.' Anna had gone on talking about other things, not realising that her mother was now drawing the dinner table again, with Dermot sitting facing the sideboard and the most important lady sitting at the other end of the table facing herself.

'Are you all right, Mother?,' Anna asked. Anna used to call her 'Mum' but now she said 'Mother'. She said it in a slightly jokey tone as if she had been saying Your Ladyship, it was if the word Mother were equally unsuitable.

'I'm fine, dear,' said Carmel. It irritated her when people asked was she all right. She never asked anyone else were they all right, even when they sounded most odd or distrait. Everyone felt they could patronise her, and pat her on the head. Even her own daughter.

'Oh good, you sounded a bit vague as if you'd gone off somewhere. Anyway, as I said, we're off to the cottage at the weekend so you'll have to tell me how the great entertaining went. I'm glad you and Dad are having people round. It's good to see you stirring yourself to do something.'

Carmel wondered again why Dermot could still be 'Dad' and not 'Father', and why it was good to be stirring herself. Why should things be stirred? Particularly, why should people be stirred? They should be left to simmer or cool down or even grow a crust on top of them if they wanted to. She said none of this to her eldest daughter.

'Oh no dear, the dinner party isn't this weekend. It's in a month's time . . . I was just thinking ahead.'

Anna burst out laughing. 'Mother, you *are* full of surprises. A month ahead! Not even James would insist on that much planning. Anyway, we'll have plenty of time to talk about it before then.' She made it sound like basketwork in an occupational therapy ward. Carmel hid her annoyance and hoped they would have a nice weekend. The weather forecast was good, and especially in the south-west.

She thought that Anna and James were quite insane to drive two hundred and nine miles on a Friday afternoon and the same distance again on Sunday. She could see no point in having a house and garden out in Sandycove and never getting to spend a weekend there. The cottage in Kerry had been an albatross around their necks as far as Carmel could see. She never believed that they could enjoy the five hour drive. 'Four hours thirty-five minutes, Grandmama, if you know the short cuts . . . ' James always made her feel even more foolish with his Grandmama; she felt like a grand duchess. But still Anna never complained, she spoke of it eagerly: 'Oh Mother, it's so great, we get there around nine-thirty and light a fire, take out the steaks, open the wine, kiddies half asleep already, pop them into bed . . . it's so free . . . the country . . . our own place . . . you can't believe it.'

Anna had heard the weather forecast too. 'Yes I am glad, because we're having a huge lunch there on Sunday and it will be so much nicer if we can have them all out of doors.'

A huge lunch, down at that cottage, in the wilds of Kerry, miles from her kitchen, her deep freeze, her dishwasher. No wonder Anna must think her pathetic worrying about seating people at a dinner party a whole month away. But of course Anna didn't have the same kind of worries. Anna would never let herself get into a situation where she would have those kind of worries.

Carmel drew the table plan again. She wrote in the names of the guests carefully. At one end of the table with her back to the window she wrote Carmel, and at the opposite end she wrote out Ruth O'Donnell,

Most Important Lady. She filled in the other names and wrote things under them too. Dermot, Loving Husband. Sheila, Wise Friend. Ethel, Upper Class Friend. Martin, Kind Husband of Wise Friend. David, Pompous Husband of Upper Class Friend. And then on the right hand side of Ruth O'Donnell she wrote, slowly and carefully, Joe, Life-Saver. She sat and looked at the plan for a long time. It stopped being a drawing of a rectangle with little squares around it holding names and descriptions. It became a table with glasses and flowers and good china and shining silver. She could almost smell the food and hear the conversation. She learned it off by heart, the order they sat in, just like she had learned the Great Lakes or the towns of Cavan when she was a child, by rote with her eyes tightly closed, relating not to things as they were but as they were written down.

Then she took all the bits of paper and put them into the firegrate. There were still a few old clinkers and some bits of red from last night's fire, but she didn't trust them to burn. She took out half a fire-lighter and set a match to it. And there in the room where she would give the party in a month's time, she sat and watched the flames burn the lists and the table plans. They burned away until there were only powdery ashes left on top of yesterday's clinkers.

*   *   *

'I think Carmel Murray is losing her marbles,' said Ethel at breakfast.

David grunted. He was reading his own letters and he did not want to be distracted by Ethel's chat.

'No seriously, listen to this . . . ' Ethel went back to the start of the letter.

'In a moment, Ethel . . . '

'No, you'll just leap up and go off, I want you to hear.'

He looked at her and knew he might as well give in. Ethel got her way in everything, and it made for an easy life to accept this.

'Carmel has lost her marbles? Go on from there.'

'Well, she must have. She's written to us. Written to ask us to dinner . . . next *month* . . . can you believe it?'

'Well, that's nice of her,' said David vaguely. 'I suppose we can get out of it, what's the fuss, what's so mad about that? People do ask each other to dinner. They do it all the time.'

He knew he was courting trouble to try and be smartalecky with Ethel. He was right; it had been a mistake.

'I know people do it all the time, dear,' she said. 'But Carmel Murray has never done it before. Poor Carmel that we have to be nice to because Dermot's a good sort . . . that's why it's unusual. And did you ever hear of anything so strange? A letter when she only lives five minutes away, when she may have heard of the telephone.'

'Yes, yes. It is odd. I do agree. You must do what you wish, say we're away, say it's a pity . . . some other time. What?'

'She'll know we're not away. That's what's so odd, it's on the day of Ruth O'Donnell's exhibition, she'll know that we won't be out of town for that . . .'

'How do you know it's that day?'

'Because she says so in the letter . . . she says that she's asked Ruth as well. Now do you see why I think she's losing her marbles?'

Ethel looked flushed and triumphant, having

proved her point. She sat imperiously at the breakfast table wearing her silk breakfast kimono and waited for the apology from her husband. It came.

'She's inviting Ruth . . . Oh my God. Now I see what you mean.'

*　　　*　　　*

Sheila hated being disturbed at school. It made the nuns so edgy and uneasy to call someone to the telephone. They hadn't moved into the modern age in terms of communications, their telephone was still in a cold and draughty little booth in the main entrance hall, inconvenient for everyone. She was alarmed when she heard that her husband wanted her . . .

'Martin, what is it, what's happened?' she said.

'Nothing. Nothing, relax.'

'What do you mean, nothing? What is it?'

'Stop fussing, Sheila, it's nothing.'

'You brought me the whole way down here from third years for nothing? Sister Delia is looking after them as a great favour. What IS it, Martin? Are the children . . . ?'

'Look, I thought you ought to know, we've had a very odd letter from Carmel.'

'A what . . . from Carmel?'

'A letter. Yes, I know it's sort of out of character, I thought maybe something might be wrong and you'd need to know . . . '

'Yes, well, what did she say, what's the matter with her?'

'Nothing, that's the problem, she's inviting us to dinner.'

'To dinner?'

'Yes, it's sort of funny, isn't it? As if she wasn't

well or something. I thought you should know in case she got in touch with you.'

'Did you really drag me all the way down here, third years are at the top of the house you know, I thought the house had burned down! God, wait till I come home to you. I'll murder you.'

'The dinner's in a month's time, and she says she's invited Ruth O'Donnell.'

'Oh, Jesus Christ.'

*   *   *

Henry shouted out to Joe, 'Hey, that letter's come from Ireland. She must have fixed the date, poor old bat.'

Joe came in and opened it.

'Yeah, in a month's time, she says it's all going according to plan. She sent the ticket and the money.'

'She's all right, isn't she?' Henry sounded approving.

'Oh, she's really fine, and I owe her, I owe her in a big way. I'll make it work .. '

'Well, if you can't, I don't know who could,' Henry said admiringly and Joe smiled back as he fetched the coffee percolator.

*   *   *

"I think Mother's coming out of herself a bit more, darling,' Anna said to James as they negotiated the early evening traffic.

'Good. It's no wonder this country's going to the dogs. Look at the build-up of traffic here and it's not even four o'clock. I mean half of them must be taking the whole afternoon off. Never mind, we'll lose them in a few minutes. What were you saying about Grandmama?'

'She's talking of having a dinner party, you know, with a proper dining table, and a seating plan. It all sounds good.'

'I've always said that she's not nearly so sleepy and dozey as you and Bernadette make out. I find plenty of things to talk to her about.'

'No you don't, you just talk at her ... she sits enthralled because you're so interesting, but it's not a real conversation.'

James didn't agree. 'You're wrong, she tells me things. No, I can't remember anything immediately ... that's silly, looking for examples. But I do get on well with her ... she just needs a bit of flattery, a few cheerful things. 'You look very dishy, Grandmama' and she blossoms ... she doesn't like people telling her she's silly.'

Anna thought for a while.

'I suppose people do tell her she's silly. Yes, you're right. I always say "Don't be silly Mother", but I don't mean it. It's just that she fusses so much, and I think that if I say she's not to be silly, then it's sort of reassuring to her. I'll be very supportive about her poor old dinner party ... I'll give her a tactful hand here and there.'

James patted her knee.

'You're marvellous, sweetheart. And talking about parties, tell me what you've arranged for Sunday ..'

Anna settled back happily in her seat and told him about all the good things that were foil-wrapped, vacuum-packed and air-tight in the huge cardboard box which they had loaded carefully into the boot of the car.

14

*　　　*　　　*

Bernadette said, 'That's great, Mummy. Great. I'm sure it will be marvellous.'

'I just thought you'd like to know . . . ' Carmel said.

'Well, of course I'm thrilled, Mummy. Is it tonight, or when?'

'Oh no dear, it's a dinner party . . . it's not for a month.'

'A *month*! Mummy, are you all right?'

'Yes dear, perfectly.'

'Oh. Well. I mean, is there anything . . . do you want me to come and help you plan it, or anything?'

'No, no, it's all planned.'

'Or serve it? You know, keep you calm and stop you fussing on the night?'

'No no, dear, thank you, but I won't fuss at all.'

'Well that's great, Mummy, and is Daddy pleased that you're sort of getting into entertaining and everything?'

'It's not exactly getting into entertaining . . . it's just one dinner party.'

'You know what I mean. Is Daddy thrilled?'

'I haven't told him yet.'

'Mummy, are you sure you're all right, you're not getting upset or anything like . . . '

'Like what, dear?'

'Like that time when you *did* get upset.'

'Oh no, dear, of course I'm not. That was when I had the trouble with my sleep patterns, they got out of kilter . . . No, that's all totally cured, thank God, now. You know that, Bernadette dear. I sleep like a log these nights. No no, that's not come back at all, thank heavens.'

Bernadette sounded troubled.

15

'No, well, good. You have to look after yourself, Mummy. You know the way you fuss about silly things, I don't want you fussing about this party . . . '

'You don't understand, child, I'm looking forward to it.'

'Good, oh and we'll come and see you soon, it's been ages.'

'Whenever you can, dear. Ring first though, I'll be out a lot in the next few weeks . . . '

'Will you, Mummy? Where?

'Here and there, dear. Anyway, it will be great to see you. How's Frank?'

'He's fine, Mummy. Take care of yourself, won't you?'

'Yes, Bernadette. Thank you, dear.'

*   *   *

Dermot thought that Carmel was a hundred miles away that morning. Twice he had said that he might be late and not to worry if he dropped into the golf club on the way home. He had to have a few chats and that was the best place to have them. Twice she had nodded amiably and distantly as if she hadn't really heard or understood.

'Will you be all right? What are you going to do today?' he had asked, uncharacteristically.

She had smiled. 'Funny you should ask that. I was just thinking that I hadn't anything to do all day so I was going to stroll down town and look at the shops. I was thinking that it was almost a sinful thing to do . just idling away the day. . . '

Dermot had smiled back. 'You're entitled to be that sinful, enjoy yourself. And as I said, if I'm late I won't want anything to eat. We might go and have a steak . . . you know. Don't fuss, don't go to any trouble.'

'No, that's fine,' she had said.

As he sat in the traffic on Morehampton Road listening to the fool on RTE telling him exactly what he knew, that Morehampton Road was blocked solid, Dermot had a vague sense of unease about Carmel. But he shook himself and decided to put it out of his mind.

'I'm becoming quite neurotic,' he told himself. 'If she does hound me about my movements and tell me detail by detail the trivia of her day I become annoyed. Now I'm uneasy because she doesn't. Impossible to please me.' He decided that everyone was being too bright on Radio Eireann and turned to the BBC where they were more solemn and in keeping with a man's thoughts in the morning as he drove in to his office.

* * *

Ruth O'Donnell hadn't got her invitation because she was away. She had gone to a farmhouse in Wales for a complete rest. She could have gone to an Irish farmhouse, but she wanted to be sure that she didn't meet anyone she knew. It wouldn't be a complete rest if she met people. She wanted to be absolutely on her own.

* * *

Carmel waited until the end of the Gay Byrne show. During the Living Word she put on her coat and took out her shopping basket on wheels. She never liked to miss Gay; once she had been able to give him a small cooker for a one-parent family. She hadn't spoken to him himself but the girl on the show had been very nice, and they had sent a nice girl to collect it, or else she was from the organisation which had asked for it. It had never been made quite clear. Carmel had sent in one or two entries for the mystery voice competition too, but she had never been called on to guess it. She didn't like to leave the house before the Living Word. It seemed rude to God, to walk out just when the few short minutes of religion were on.

She knew she should really listen to programmes like Day by Day which followed it, they would make her informed, but somehow she always felt her mind wandering and she never quite understood why people got so hot under the collar about things. Once she had said to Sheila that it would be nice to have someone sitting beside you to tell you what was going on in life, and Sheila told her to shut up, otherwise everyone would say they had learned nothing after all those years with the Loreto nuns . . . She thought that Sheila had been upset that day but she couldn't be sure.

It was bright and sunny out, a nice autumn day. She pushed her tartan shopping bag on wheels in front of her, remembering when it had been a pram that she pushed. She used to know many more people in those days. She was always stopping and talking to people, wasn't she? Or was that memory playing tricks, like thinking that the summers were always hot when she was young and that they had spent their whole time on Killiney beach? That wasn't true, her younger brother Charlie said that they only went twice or three times a summer; perhaps the other memory wasn't true either. Perhaps she didn't stop at the bottom of Eglinton Road when she pointed out to the girls where the buses went to sleep in the bus home, perhaps there had been nobody much around then either.

She looked at the prices of wine in the off-licence and wrote down the names of some of them so that she could make her list and selection later on. She then spent a happy hour looking at books in the big book shop. She copied down recipe after recipe in her little jotter. From time to time she got a look from one of the assistants, but she looked respectable and was causing no trouble so nobody said anything. Seared in her mind was a remark that Ethel had once made about a house where she had dined. 'The woman has no imagination. I can't understand why you ask people round for prawn cocktail and roast beef . . . I mean, why not tell them to eat at home and come round later for drinks?' Carmel loved prawn cocktail, and had little glass dishes which it would look very well in. They used to have trifle in them when she was young. She had kept them after things had been divided up between herself and Charlie but she had never used them. They stood gathering dust, eight of them, at the back of the cupboard in the scullery. She would make another kind of starter, not prawn cocktail, and she would use those selfsame glasses for it, whatever it was. She rejected grapefruit segments and worked it out methodically. You couldn't have paté, that would have to be on a plate, or soup, that couldn't be in a glass, or any kind of fish of course . . . no, it had to be something cold you ate with a spoon.

She would find it eventually, she had all day, she had twenty-nine more days . . . there was no rush. She must not get fussed. She found it. Orange Vinaigrette.

19

Ethel couldn't say that that was unimaginative . . . you cut up oranges and black olives and onions and fresh mint . . . sounded terrific, you poured a vinaigrette sauce over it . . . it would be perfect. Carmel smiled happily. She knew that she was doing the right thing. All she had to do was go at it slowly.

She would go home now and rest; tomorrow she would come out and find a main course, and then a dessert. She had work to do at home too. Joe had said that if he was going to come and help her he would need co-operation. She mustn't have turned into a dowdy middle-aged old frump, she must look smart and glamorous and well-turned-out. She had thirty afternoons to organise that.

*   *   *

Sheila dropped in on her way home from school. She seemed relieved to find Carmel there, and there was a look of worry on her face.

'I was a little alarmed, Martin told me you had sent us a letter.'

'It was only an invitation,' Carmel smiled. 'Come on in and we'll have a coffee. I was in the middle of tidying out some cupboards .. I've a lot of clothes that should go to the Vincent de Paul . . . but you know what always happens, you're ashamed to give them the way they are, so you get them cleaned first. Then when they come back from the cleaners they're better than anything else you have in the press so you never give them at all.' Carmel laughed happily as they went into the kitchen and put on the kettle.

'It just seemed so funny to write, when I talk to you nearly every day . . . '

'Did it? Oh, I don't know, I'm such a bad hostess I

thought you have to write things down as invitations or people didn't believe you. I suppose that's why I wrote. I'd have told you anyway.'

'But you didn't tell me yesterday.'

'No, I must have forgotten.'

'There's nothing wrong, is there, Carmel? You *are* all right?'

Carmel had her back to Sheila. She deliberately relaxed her shoulders and refused to clench her fists. Nobody was going to see just how annoyed she became when people asked her in that concerned tone whether she was all right.

'Sure I am, why wouldn't I be, a lady of leisure? It's you who must be exhausted coping with all that noise and those demons all day. I think you should be canonised.'

'Tell me about the dinner party,' Sheila said.

'Oh, it's not for a month yet,' Carmel laughed.

'I know.' Sheila's patience seemed strained. 'I know it's not for a month, but you actually put pen to paper and wrote so I thought it was a big thing.'

'No no, just eight of us, I said it in the letter.'

'Yes, Martin told me, I wasn't at home when it arrived.'

'He rang you? Oh, isn't he good. There was no need to. I mean you could have told me any time.'

'Yes, and you could have told *me* any time.' Sheila looked worried.

'Yes, of course. Heavens, we are both making a production of it! When you think how many parties Ethel goes to, and indeed gives . . . '

'Yes, well, Ethel is Ethel.'

'And you, I mean you and Martin often have people round, don't you? I often hear you say you had people in.'

'Yes, but that's very casual.'

'Oh, this will be too. Mainly people we all know well.'

'But Ruth . . . Ruth O'Donnell . . . we don't know her all that well, and honestly, do you know, I think that's the night that her exhibition opens — in fact I'm sure of it.'

'Yes, I know it is, I said that in the letter. Didn't Martin tell you? So I know we'll all be going to it . . . but it's at four o'clock . . . it will be well over by six, and even if people go to have a drink afterwards . . . well, they're not invited here until eight, for half past.'

'Yes, but don't you think on the night of her own exhibition she might want to go out with her own friends?'

'But we're her friends, in a way.'

'Not really, are we? I mean, are you? She doesn't normally come here?'

'No, I don't think she's ever been here. I thought it would be nice for her . . . and she doesn't live far away, in that new block of flats, so she won't have far to go to change.'

Sheila put down her mug of coffee.

'I don't think it's a good idea. We don't know her. Why ask someone we don't know very well to a dinner? Let's just have the six of us . . . it would be more friendly.'

'No, I've asked her anyway, and I can't think what you say that for. You're the one who tells me to go out and meet more people.'

'I didn't tell you to go out and invite well-known artists to dinner,' muttered Sheila.

'Don't lecture me,' Carmel said with a laugh, and Sheila had to admit to herself that Carmel did look

22

more cheerful and like herself than she had in the last while. She looked a bit more like the Carmel of the old days.

'All right, I won't. Let me see your cupboard cleaning. Maybe you could give something to me instead of the Vincent de Paul. I could do with it. A teacher doesn't get paid much, God help us, when you consider how we put our lives at risk.'

'How's Martin feeling?'

'Oh, he's fine. He's great, you know, he never complains. I'm sure he's fed up but he never complains.' Martin had been made redundant two years ago when two firms had merged. He had got a golden handshake. He was still only fifty-two and he expected to get another job, then he expected to write a book. Everybody else thought he was writing a book, but Sheila never lied to Carmel. To Carmel she admitted that Martin was doing the hoovering and the shopping. They pretended that Sheila loved being back in the classroom. Not many people knew how much she hated it. Her children didn't know, not even Martin really knew. Carmel sometimes suspected, but Carmel was a long-time friend It didn't matter what she knew. It was just a bit worrying sometimes the things she did. Like inviting that woman to dinner. Was there a possibility that Carmel's nerves were bad again? She sounded so well, and she looked fine. But it *was* the act of a madwoman.

'Hey, you are doing a thorough job. You've taken everything out. Which is the good pile and which is the bad pile?'

'I don't know, they all seem the same. They're like mouse clothes, aren't they? Do you remember when we went to pantomimes years and years ago? People were dressed in mouse outfits and rat outfits . . . that's what these are like!'

'Carmel, you are preposterous! Of course your clothes aren't like that, they're smashing. Have you two of these blue cardigans?'

'I think I've three of them. Whenever I go to a shop I can never think of anything to buy except grey skirts and blue cardigans. Have one of each.'

'I mean it. Quite, quite preposterous.'

Carmel smiled happily. Other people said 'Don't be silly'; Sheila said she was preposterous. It was much, much nicer.

*   *   *

'Well?' Martin wanted to know.

'I *think* she's all right. It's hard to know.'

'You mean it was a joke about the invitation?'

'No, she means it. She's having the party, she just doesn't want to talk about it.'

'Then she's not all right.'

'I know, but she *seems* normal. She gave me a skirt and a cardigan.'

'That makes her normal?'

'No, you know what I mean. She was talking about ordinary things. She hadn't gone off on any flight of fancy or anything . . . '

'So did you talk her out of it?' Martin wanted to know.

'I couldn't, she wouldn't talk about it at all. I *told* you.'

'Oh great,' he sighed. 'That's all we need. You're her friend, for Christ's sake.'

'Martin, I've had a bad day. Not just a bit of a bad day — every single bit of it was bad. I don't want to talk about it any more. I did my best to talk to

Carmel, she wouldn't talk back, that's all. Can't you leave me alone!'

'Yes, I know I should have had a drink ready and the fire lighting and tried to soothe away your cares . . like a proper housewife. I'm sorry I'm bad at it. You don't have to tell me.'

'Jesus, Martin, if this is the night you've picked to do a wretched "I'm not a good provider" act, then you've picked the wrong night. Will you shut up and sit down. I love you, I don't want you to fart around pandering to me just because *my* outfit didn't close down . . . do you hear me?'

He was contrite.

'I'm sorry. I really am. I'm just worried, that's all.'

'So am I.'

'Do you think she knows about Ruth? Do you think she heard anything . . . ?'

'How could she have heard anything? Who does she meet? Where does she go? Unless it was on the Gay Byrne Hour or in the Evening Press Diary she'd not have heard.'

'What are we going to do?'

'I haven't a clue.'

*　　　*　　　*

'I'm sorry I'm late,' called David. 'The traffic was bloody terrible. There's no point in taking a car in these days, I've said it over and over.'

'So have I, the number ten would take you to your door.'

'I can't travel on the number ten. It never comes, or it's full when it does.'

'Anyway, why buy a big car and not show it off?'

'What?' David sounded bad-tempered in the hall.

'Nothing. You said you're sorry you're late, get a move on then, if you want to change or wash or anything . . . '

'For what?' David sounded even crosser. 'Oh God, I'd forgotten. Do we have to? Can't we . . . ?'

'We *do* have to and we *can't* ring and say we're tied up. We accepted two weeks ago.'

'It's all very well for you.' David was pounding up the stairs crossly. 'You have nothing to do all day but get yourself ready . . . titivate . . . titivate.'

'Thank you,' Ethel said icily.

She sat at the dressing table in their bedroom. The door to the bathroom was open and he could see the thick coloured towels piled up on the chest of drawers. He knew he would feel much better when he had a bath, he knew it was unfair to blame her.

'I'm sorry,' he said.

He kissed her at the dressing table. She smelled whiskey.

'Do they serve cocktails in traffic jams?' she asked.

He laughed. 'You've caught me out. I dropped into the club.' He looked contrite.

'Which is of course on the route home.' She was still cold.

'No, of course it wasn't, but I took the lower road. Oh hell, I only had two, but do you know who was there? You'll never guess what happened.'

She was interested. He rarely told tales of interest from the outer world; she had to prod and pry and ferret to find out anything that might be happening. She followed him into the bathroom. He flung off his coat and struggled with his shirt.

'I met Dermot, Dermot Murray.'

'Oh yes?' She was as sharp as a hawk now, pique forgotten. 'What did he say?'

'Well, it's amazing, it's quite amazing.'

'Yes? Yes?'

'He was sitting talking to some fellows, I don't know who they were. I've seen one of them, perfectly respectable, in the property business, I think, out the Northside . . . anyway, he was in that corner place with them.'

'Yes . . . what did he say?'

'Wait, wait, I'm telling you.' David had run the bath as he was speaking. The water gushed with powerful pressure from each tap, the room had steamed up in under a minute.

'I said to him, "How are you, Dermot?"'

David stood in his underpants tantalising his wife by the meticulous way he was repeating the trivia of the conversation. She decided not to be drawn.

'I'll sit on the loo here and when you feel like telling me, do.'

He pulled the shower curtains around him when he got into the bath. This was a modesty that had grown somewhere around the same time as his paunch. When they had been younger they had often bathed together, and had always bathed in front of each other.

'No, it's really strange,' came the voice from inside the curtain. 'I said "Thanks very much for that invitation," and he said "What invitation?" and I got such a shock I started to play the fool. You know. I said, "Come on now. You can't welch on us now, an invite's an invite."'

'What did he say then?'

'He said, "You have me on the wrong foot, David. I don't actually know what you mean." He said it so straight, I felt a bit foolish. I just got out of it. I said that I had probably made a mistake, or that you

27

hadn't looked at the letter properly.'

'Thank you very much again,' said Ethel.

'I had to say something. Anyway he said, "Letter, what letter?" I was right into it then. I said, "Oh, it's some mistake. I thought we'd got a letter from you and Carmel inviting us to dinner. I must have got it wrong." He said it wasn't very likely that she'd have invited people without telling him. Maybe it was a surprise party.'

'Boy, some surprise if it is!' said Ethel.

'That's what I thought, so I said the date. I said it's on the eighth. He said, "Well I never. Maybe it's all a birthday treat and I'm not meant to know." But he looked worried. He said, "the eighth", again, as if it was familiar. Then he said, "Not the eighth?" And I said, nervously you know, "I'm sure I got it wrong" . . .'

'He doesn't know. She's doing it without telling him. She's asking us all round there for some kind of terrible drama. That's what it's all about.' Ethel's face looked stricken rather than excited. It should be an exciting thing . . . a public row, a scandal. But not with Carmel Murray. Poor Carmel, she was too vulnerable.

David got out of the bath and dried himself vigorously in one of the big yellow towels.

'He really doesn't know she's giving the party, the poor devil. Isn't that a dreadful thing? Thank God I said something, even though I felt I had walked into it. At least it will give him a bit of time to know what action to take.'

'But she can't know about Ruth, she can't possibly know.' Ethel was thoughtful.

'Somebody may have sent her a poison pen letter — you know, "I think you ought to know" . . .' David was still towelling himself dry.

'You'll rub the skin off your back. Come on, get dressed. She can't know. If she knew would she in a million years ask her to dinner?'

*   *   *

Joe and Henry were cooking for a party. They often did home catering; it was very easy money. They made the canapés while they watched television, and put everything in the freezer. They got lots of free perks like clingfilm and foil from the hotel where Henry worked, and the use of a car from the tourist guide service where Joe worked.

'Why won't the old bat let you do the cooking for her if she's so nervous? You could run up a dinner in two hours.'

'No, that's part of it. She has to be able to do it all herself.'

'What does she look like? All sad and mopey, is she?'

'I don't know,' said Joe. 'I haven't seen her for twenty years. She may have changed a lot since then.'

*   *   *

'Hallo, Carmel, is that you?'

'Of course it is, love, who else would it be?'

'Carmel, I'm at the club, I told you, I've had to have a few chats, I told you.'

'I know you told me.'

'So I won't be home, or I wasn't coming home. Have you had your supper?'

'Supper?'

'Carmel, it's eight o'clock. I'm ringing you from the club to ask you a simple question: have you or have you not had your supper?'

'I had some soup, Dermot, but there's steak here, and cauliflower . . . I can cook whatever you like.'

'Did you write to David?'

'WHAT? It's very hard to hear you. There's a lot of noise behind you.'

'Forget it. I'll come home.'

'Oh good. Would you like me to . . . ?'

He had hung up.

*　　　*　　　*

All the way home he said to himself it was impossible. She couldn't have decided to hold a dinner party without telling him, and if she had, if by some mind-blowing horror she had decided to invite all their friends around to witness a scene of marital bliss . . . how could she have chosen the eighth of October?

It was Ruth's birthday, her thirtieth birthday. He had persuaded her to hold her exhibition that day, to show everyone that she had arrived. Ruth had said that she wanted no public exhibitions, no showing the world anything, unless he could stand beside her. She didn't want to go on hiding and pretending. When the reporters were sent to interview her she didn't want to have to laugh any more and parry questions about why she had never married. She felt foolish telling people that her art was her life. It sounded so hollow, so second best and so phoney. She wanted to tell them that she loved and was loved. It was this that gave her strength to paint.

She had agreed reluctantly. The gallery had been found with no trouble. People were anxious to hang the work of Ruth O'Donnell. The work was ready. She was drained. She said she wanted time away, far away, from him. She would not spend the days planning how to walk out of his life, she assured him of that, and he believed her. She just wanted to be free, to rest, and not to hide. He believed that too. He promised he wouldn't telephone her, nor write. That would be the same as being with him, she said. There was no point in a separation if you spent hours writing a letter and waiting for the post.

She was coming back on the first, a full week before it opened, in time to see everything hung. She had only left yesterday. It wasn't possible that coincidence should be so cruel as to mar this night for him by having a weeping Carmel on his hands. Because by God if she had arranged a dinner party for the eighth she was going to unarrange it fast. That was why he had left those two auctioneers sitting like eejits in the club. This had to be sorted out immediately.

*   *   *

'I think Mummy's a bit lonely,' Bernadette said to Frank.

'We're all lonely. It's the lot of men and women to go through life alone thinking they are with friends but only brushing off people.'

'I mean it,' Bernadette said. 'She's very good to us, Frank. She pretends she doesn't mind about us living together but she does, underneath.'

'Nonsense. Just so long as we don't do anything too public in front of all those friends of hers, she's as right as rain.'

'All what friends of hers? There's no friends.'

'There must be. Posh house there in the heart of society . . . of course she has friends. Didn't you tell me tonight that she's organising dinner parties months in advance?'

'That's what I don't like.'

'God, there's no pleasing you! You're like a gnat; say out what you want and I'll debate whether we'll do it or not. Do you want us to kidnap her and keep her in the bathroom here tied by a dressing-gown cord for the rest of her life?'

'No,' she laughed.

'What do you want, Ber?'

'I wondered if we might drop in tonight, on our way to the party. Please.'

'Aw God,' he said.

'Just for a little bit,' she begged.

'We'll be there all night,' he said.

'We won't. We'll just get off the bus, run in and have a few words and then run off again.'

'That's worse than not going at all.'

'No, it would ease my mind.'

'Ten minutes then, right?'

'Half an hour, right?'

'Twenty minutes.'

'Done.'

*   *   *

'Don't say anything to the O'Briens about it, will you?' Ethel said when they were in the car.

'What would I say? I'm not a one for gossip, I never talk about people. You're the one who likes to tell and be told.'

David had his eyes on the road but he knew his wife's profile was stern. 'No, I'll say nothing to anyone. God, do you think we should do something or say something? We can't sit back and let it all happen.'

'What can we do that would help, heavens above? You sound like Superman or the archangel Gabriel stepping in. What can we do?'

'I suppose we could say to Carmel that it's not a good idea, that she might like to think again.'

'It's amazing how you manage to hold down a job, let alone run your own business,' said Ethel acerbically.

'It's all due to the loyal little woman behind me. She had faith in me when no one else had,' he said in a mock country and western accent.

'Well, if ever I meet the woman behind you I can tell you one thing, I'll not invite her to dinner with all our friends,' said Ethel, and they drove on to the O'Briens in silence.

*   *   *

Frank and Bernadette were just leaving when Dermot's car drew up.

'Maybe he'd give us a lift,' said Frank optimistically.

'I think that's a bit too sunny a view. I wouldn't ask him,' said Bernadette. 'How are you, Dad?'

'I see it's the annual visit,' Dermot said.

'Hi, Mr Murray,' said Frank.

'Hallo, er . . .' said Dermot desperately, stumbling over his name.

Bernadette's fist clenched in her pocket. 'We were just in having a chat with Mummy. We're off to a party.'

'Don't let me delay you,' Dermot said.

'Oh Daddy, you can be very rude,' Bernadette said. 'Why can't you be nice and easygoing, and . . . '

'I don't know,' Dermot said. 'It must be something to do with having to go out and earn a living and take on responsibilities.'

'We work too, Daddy.'

'Huh,' said Dermot.

'Nice to have talked with you, Mr Murray,' said Frank in an affected American accent.

'Sorry,' Dermot said. 'I'm in a bad mood. You do work, both of you. I'm just worried about something. Come back into the house and I'll give you a drink.'

'That's mighty white of you, sir,' said Frank.

'No Dad, we've got to be off. We just looked in to see was Mummy all right.'

'And she is, isn't she?' Dermot sounded alarmed.

'Oh yes,' Bernadette said, a little too quickly. 'She's fine.'

*　　　*　　　*

'I heard your voices. Did you meet them in the drive?' Carmel asked.

It had always irritated Dermot that she called the small distance to the gate a 'drive': it was eleven steps from the hall door to the gate if you took giant steps, and the most you could make out of it was twenty little ones.

'Yes. What did they want?'

'Oh Dermot, they just called in, it was nice of them.'

'They said they came to see were you all right. Why did they do that?'

'That's what people do, dear, when they call to see other people.'

She looked cheerful and calm. There was no resigned martyred air about her. She wasn't making little jokes which were not funny. She had no hint of tears.

'Will we have a proper meal at the table or would

you like a snack by the television?' she asked. 'The phone was so crackly and with the sound of people behind I couldn't hear whether you had a meal or you hadn't. You kept asking me had I . . . '

'Sit down, love,' he said.

'Yes, I will in a minute, but what would you . . . '

'Sit down now, Carmel. I want to talk to you, not to your back drifting out the door.'

'All right, Dermot, all right. Now will this do?'

'Have you or have you not invited a whole lot of people here on the eighth of October?'

'Certainly not.'

'You haven't?' The relief was overwhelming. It spilled all over his face. 'I'm sorry, love. There was a silly misunderstanding.'

'No. I just asked our friends and decided we'd have a nice evening and cook a nice dinner. You know you often said . . . '

'What do you mean . . . ?'

'You've often said that we should have people around more, and somehow I usen't to feel able for it, but I decided you were right, so I just asked a few people . . . for dinner.'

'When? When?'

'Oh, ages away. The eighth as you said, the eighth of October. Just a simple dinner.'

'Who have you asked?'

'Just friends. Sheila and Martin, and David and Ethel, and . . . '

'You've invited them all here on the eighth?'

'Yes. And I've asked that nice Ruth O'Donnell, you know, the artist.'

'Carmel. What are you . . . ?'

'You remember her, we met her lots of times, and

you told me how good she was. We haven't seen her for ages, but I did say when I wrote to her that there would be lots of people she'd know . . . I mean, David even knows her professionally. His company gave her a grant once, I read . . . '

'Yes . . . '

'And she'll know Sheila, because I think she came to her school to give a lecture.'

'Why didn't you ask me — tell me?'

'But, Dermot, you're always telling me to do things on my own, use my own initiative. I did for once. I sent out all the invitations . . . and now that doesn't please you either.'

'But I think you've picked the wrong night. I think that's the night she's having her opening. I thought I told you . . . '

'Yes you did, I remember. You said she was only thirty and how well she'd done. I remember the date.'

'God.'

'So I thought it would be nice for her to have somewhere to go after it. I read in the papers that she isn't married and she doesn't even have a "situation" like our Bernadette, so I thought what would be nicer than for her to have somewhere to go on the night.'

'Yes.'

'So that's what I said in my letter to her, that it would be a nice rounding off for the evening.'

'How did you know where she lives?' His voice was a gasp.

'I looked it up in the telephone directory, silly!'

'You might have sent it to the wrong person . . . '

'But she told us she lived in the new flats. Remember? I'm not such a featherbrain after all, am I?'

*　　　*　　　*

'Sheila, can I have a quick word with you before you go into the school?'

'God, you frightened the life out of me, Dermot Murray. I thought you were a guard.'

'Look, have you a minute? Can we get back into your car?'

'Half the Sixth years already think you're propositioning me! What is it, Dermot? Tell me here.'

"No, it's nothing to tell. I want to ask you, ask you something.'

Sheila's heart was leaden.

'Ask on, but make it quick. That bell rings and I'm like a bolt from the blue in the door.'

'Does Carmel know about Ruth?'

'I beg your pardon?'

'You heard me.'

'I didn't. I did *not* hear you. Begin again.'

'Does Carmel know about Ruth and me?'

'Ruth? Ruth O'Donnell?'

'Sheila, stop playing around. I know you know, you know I know you know. All I want to know is does Carmel know?'

'You're assuming a great many things. What is there to know? What should I have known? Stop standing there like a guessing game.'

'Sheila, please, it's important.'

'It must be. Why else are you up here in a convent? I haven't an idea what you're talking about.'

'Think, think quickly. I know you're being a good friend and an old school chum. But think what's for the best. I don't just mean the best for me, I mean the best for everyone.'

'What am I to think about?'

'Look, I've known you for years, Sheila, I'm not a shit, now am I? I'm a reasonable human being. Would

I be up here at this hour of the morning if I was a real bum?'

Every day that Sheila had paused at her car for one moment to search for an exercise book, to write a shopping list, to listen to the last bars of some song on the radio . . . the bell had shrilled across her consciousness. Why did it not do it today?

'I can't help you, Dermot,' she said. 'I don't know anything, I really don't. I don't talk about anything, I don't listen to anything. I'm no help.'

He believed her. Not that she didn't know about Ruth. He knew she knew about Ruth. But he believed her when she said she couldn't help him. She didn't know whether Carmel knew or not. She was as much in the dark as he was.

'What am I going to do?' he asked her.

And then the bell shrilled.

*   *   *

'I just telephoned to ask you more about this party you're giving,' Ethel said.

'I explained it all in the letter,' said Carmel. 'You will be able to come? You see I know how busy you all are so I trapped you by choosing the night of Ruth's exhibition.'

'Yes, of course we'll come. You don't have to trap us. Looking forward to it . . . I was wondering whether it was a surprise — a birthday surprise for Dermot or anything. David met him in the club, and I hope he didn't let anything slip.'

'No, it's not Dermot's birthday. It may well be Ruth's, I think hers is in October, but no, it doesn't matter at all. I did tell Dermot I was thinking of having a party, but you know what men are, they never listen. Their minds are elsewhere. Probably just as well that we don't know where they are half the time, don't you think?'

Ethel had the uneasy feeling that Carmel was laughing at her. Nonsense, of course, but there was that kind of a feel about the way she spoke.

＊　　　＊　　　＊

'Oh, Dermot, I can't tell you where she is. She said the whole point was that you and she were having a separation, wasn't it?'

'Look, I'll go down on my knees to you.'

Dermot had never liked Ruth's younger sister. A know-all, a moraliser and worst of all a contemporary of his daughter Anna's when they were at UCD.

'No, I swore I would reveal nothing. Ruth only told me just in case there was any real crisis, about the gallery, you know.'

'There's a very big crisis. I can't tell you how big.'

'Honestly, Dermot, be fair. Play it by the rules. Just leave her alone, can't you? It's only a couple of weeks.'

'Listen here, smarty pants,' Dermot had lost any veneer of manners by now. 'Go into Ruth's flat, where there will be a letter with a Dublin Four postmark addressed to her. Open it and read it. If you think then that it's serious enough perhaps you could ring your sister and ask her to ring me. That's all.' He stood up to leave the travel agency where she worked.

'Wait. It's not some awful sordid thing . . . some scandal, is it?' The girl's lip wrinkled with disgust.

'It's only a dinner invitation, but she might want to ring me about it.'

He nearly took the door off the hinges as he left.

*　　　*　　　*

Dermot telephoned his office.

'Oh there you are, Mr Murray,' the girl on the switch said with relief. 'It's not like you to be late. I didn't know what to do with your calls. We've had . . . '

'I'm not feeling well today, Margaret. Kindly inform the manager, and ask Miss O'Neill to put someone else on the Foreign Exchange and move her own things to my desk.'

'But Mr Murray . . . '

'I'll call back later, Margaret. The important thing is that Miss O'Neill sits at my desk. Put any calls for me through to her, she will know how to deal with them.'

'When will you . . . ?'

'As I said, I'll call back later, Margaret. The bank is not going to grind to a halt just because for once the manager isn't well.'

He hung up and regretted it immediately. The child on the switch didn't care whether the bank ground to a halt or not. Probably hoped it would if the truth was known. Why had he been so snappy, she was bound to gossip about it too. If only he had just taken thirty more seconds to be soothing and reassuring then it would have passed unnoticed in the minutiae of the day . . . poor Mr Murray's not well, must have that bug, oh well, Miss O'Neill's looking after his work . . . and that would be that. Now the girl on the switch would be full of indignation . . . bit my nose off, snapped at me over nothing, all I was doing was asking, what do I bloody care where he is, what he does, he can take a running jump at himself.

Why couldn't he have had the patience to exchange just two more conventional remarks? He had been so patient, so very patient about everything so far. Why couldn't he have kept his temper this morning? He frowned at his reflection in the car mirror when he got back into the driving seat. He didn't like the middle-aged tense man that looked back at him. In his mind's eye he didn't see himself that way; in his mind's eye he saw himself as Ruth's man, her strong support, the one she ran to when she was exhausted with her work, when she was full of doubts. To the little girl on the switch back at the bank, he was probably middle-aged Mr Murray, and if she knew about Ruth (which she might well in this village that they called a city) then she would think he was pathetic with his bit on the side, or a louse cheating on his wife.

Dermot didn't feel like driving anywhere. He got out of the car again and walked until he reached the canal. It was a nice crisp morning. Other people were still in their cars choking with fumes. These must be big executives, the top men, if they could come in to work as late as ten to ten, or was that right? If they were top men maybe they should have been at their desks since seven-thirty? Maybe they were the kind of men who had inherited a family business and who didn't have to work hard because they were the bosses' sons. Funny how you saw different sides of society when you stepped off your own little treadmill for a bit.

Two women passed him on the canal path, bright laughing women in headscarfs. One was carrying a huge plastic bag and the other a large stuffed pillowcase; they were on their way to the launderette. They were the kind of women that Carmel would describe as nice poor things. And yet they weren't nearly as poor as poor Carmel. They were carting their families' washing off without a look of resentment about them. Carmel might be bending over the controls of a washing machine in her own kitchen but more likely she would just sit and stare out into the back garden. He had looked at her in off-guard moments over the last few months and this was how she was when in repose. Her face was empty as if she had left it and gone somewhere else.

He had hoped she would find interests, but he realised more and more that this was a vain hope. She had no interests. She had nothing whatsoever that would lift her out of that sad pose. When Anna and James had had the first baby Dermot thought that this would absorb Carmel's time, a grandchild out in Sandycove. He was certain she would be out there every second day, or encouraging Anna to leave the child in Donnybrook while she went about her business. But Dermot hadn't understood about modern young mothers like Anna. Cilian first, and then Orla, had just become part of her own life as if they were adults. They were constantly being strapped and unstrapped into car seats. They moved with a battery of educational toys, they were quite self-sufficient wherever they went. Doting grandmothers did not come into the picture at all.

And then of course that strap Bernadette shacked up with that Frank; 'my flat mate,' no less, she called him. She hadn't been much help or support for her mother, had she? Dermot muttered to himself about her. A lot of use it had been paying for her at the College of Art, quite happy to help friends out, to step in and sell things for someone who was stuck.

And friends? Carmel was a great one for talking about the Girls. Where were the girls now when they were needed? That Sheila, the schoolmistress rushing into the convent this morning as if her life depended on it. Great friend she'd be if anyone needed one; 'I don't talk, I don't listen, I don't know things . . .' marvellous! And who else was there? There was Ethel . . . she and Carmel had got on quite well at one stage. But there as well as anywhere else Carmel hadn't been able to cope. She had talked and talked about not returning David and Ethel's hospitality, and not accepting any more of it. Why hadn't she just said 'Come around to supper,' the way Ruth did, the way anyone did . . . anyone except Carmel.

It was fooling himself really to think she would be happier without him, fooling himself to say she wouldn't really notice if he left. She would not be able to cope. She couldn't even muster the politics of solidarity and hate, like that woman they had heard of in Ballsbridge, the wife of the man in the public relations agency. She had been so outraged when he left that she had aligned dozens of women on her side. You could hardly mention the man's name now without hearing a sibilant hiss, so blackened had it become. No, Carmel would do nothing like that.

Dermot stopped suddenly. Carmel would do nothing. And that was why he could never leave her. She would do nothing at all. For the rest of his life he would come home, tell lies, make up excuses, invent conferences, be telephoned by mythical clients who had to be seen after hours. And Ruth would do nothing. Ruth would not make a scene, demand that he choose between them, Ruth would confront nobody, insist on no showdowns. This had been the way things were for two whole years . . . everyone secure in the knowledge that nobody else would do anything; Ruth knowing she would never have to make her mind up about him fully, Carmel knowing that she would never lose him utterly and he knowing that he need never be forced to say 'I'll take this one' or 'I'll take that.'

He laughed wryly to himself. It was most people's idea of a married man's dream: an unquestioning wife and an unquestioning mistress. But it was a bad dream, he could write a book on what a bad dream it was. You were happy in neither place, you were guilty in both places. The very fact that nobody was making any move made it all the more insoluble. If Carmel had threatened and pleaded, perhaps, if Ruth had issued ultimatums, perhaps. *Perhaps* it might have been better. But nothing ever happened. Until now. Until Ruth had been invited to dinner.

*   *   *

Carmel *must* know, he said to himself for the five hundredth time. She *must* know. And yet the memory of last night had been like a vivid movie running through over and over.

'Tell me, why have you decided to ask Ruth O'Donnell whom we hardly know, whom you only met twice, to dinner? Carmel, what are you playing at?'

'I'm not playing at anything except being a better homemaker. She's nice. Everyone says so.'

'But why? Tell me, what made you think of a dinner? Why a month away?'

'To give me time to prepare to get ready. I'm not like all these marvellous women you admire so much who can have the entire golf game round for a six-course meal with no notice. I like to take my time.'

She had looked at him with a round innocent face.

She had prattled on about Sheila having called in, about Anna and James driving off to the cottage, about how she wished she could get the Christmas presents months ahead in September when the shops were nice and empty.

Four times he asked her in a roundabout way, four times she had answered him with a level look. She just liked the idea of having people to dinner; why was he finding fault with it? And he never answered that question, not even with a lie.

*   *   *

They went to Mass at eleven o'clock in Donnybrook church and bought the papers outside.

'Do you need anything from the shops?' Dermot asked. 'Ice cream? a pudding?'

'No, I'm on a diet, but you get some if you like,' she said pleasantly. He had looked at her face as she prayed; he had watched her come back from Communion with her head down. She never asked him why he didn't go to Communion, she never asked him anything.

*   *   *

Anna and James were happy. It had been a glorious day and they had had their lunch out in the open. Twelve of them had sat and looked out over the bay and said that this was the life and they must all be mad to live in Dublin. Anna had arranged that a local woman make fresh soda bread and they had had this with their paté. Everyone had raved about it. Cilian and Orla played at a distance with the three visiting children. Some of their friends had been staying at an hotel, others had rented a cottage . . . they all looked with open envy at the ease and comfort which James and Anna had built for themselves. This was balm to Anna and James. They stood and waved in the evening as the last guests drove off, they had cups of tea to get rid of the sleepiness the white wine had spread, and they looked at the clock. James had an iron rule: on the road back at seven. This meant an hour to wash up and tidy and pack the children and themselves — plenty of time.

They moved around the cottage gathering the bagful of educational toys. They plunged their twelve plates, twelve glasses, twelve forks and twelve knives into the hot soapy water. A rubbish sack was collected, carefully tied up and put in the boot as well. There were no dustmen in this part of heaven, they laughed to each other. Cilian and Orla, sleepy from the day in the sun, were strapped in, the cassette of James Last was at the ready and they faced the road across the country.

They spent much of it congratulating each other on the cottage. Although they would never have admitted it, even to each other, there were times when they thought it was becoming a bit much for them. But on a day like today when they could see the admiration and the jealousy of the people who sat around in the sunshine, then it was all worth it a hundred times over. They forgot the weekends they had arrived to find pipes burst, roof leaking, ants walking the kitchen floor in their thousands, mice making nests in the window boxes . . . all that was as nothing. The strings of the Last orchestra thudded and swept in the background.

James said: 'Do you know that your father's having an affair with Ruth O'Donnell, the artist?'

'Dad? Don't be ridiculous.'

'He is though, I heard it before. I heard it from someone who met them in London, of all places. Wouldn't you think you'd be safe having it away in London, ten million people, but no, spotted in flagrante.'

Anna looked around almost automatically to see if the children were asleep. If their grandfather's adultery was going to be discussed it would not be devant these enfants, she thought.

'I don't believe a word of it.'

'Honestly, sweetheart, Frances and Tim were talking about it this afternoon. They didn't like to mention it in front of you.'

'So that's what you were wittering on about. I thought it was business.'

'No, they tell me they see him often coming out of Ruth's apartment block, you know.'

'The new one . . . yes . . . heavens above.'

'Are you upset, are you upset that I told you?'

'I don't believe it, not *Dad*. I mean, he fancies her maybe and goes in and has the odd little drink. But not an affair, not sleeping with her, not Dad.'

'Um.'

'Well, don't you agree?'

'I don't know, I only tell you what I hear.'

'You think it's possible that Dad would have a real affair?'

'That's what is said.'

'But why would she? I mean she's young and well known and got her own life . . . she could have anyone or no one if she wanted. What on earth would she want with Dad?'

'Who knows? People want extraordinary people.'

'Yes.'

'You are upset. I shouldn't have told you like that straight out. It's just . . . well, it was on my mind.'

'I'm not upset. I don't know why. I suppose when I was young like everyone I was always terrified if they had a row that they were going to part. But they didn't, nobody ever did. Things just go along drifting. That's what happened to marriages in those days.'

'And in *these* days, it would appear.'

'What do you mean?'

'Well, they say that your Papa and Ms. O'Donnell have been constant companions for two to three years.'

'Never!'

'Apparently.'

'Imagine at Christmas, and the year before and the year before . . . all the family party . . . and all the time . . . I don't believe it.'

'Do you think Grandmama knows?'

'I'm certain she doesn't. Poor Mother. How odd, I don't know why I'm not all crying and thinking it's the end of everything. I suppose I just haven't accepted it.'

'I don't know why I told you.' James looked worried. 'It's only making you sad, but it seemed a big secret to keep from you . . . we don't have secrets.'

'No.'

'And you're so practical, I thought you'd want to know about it in case there's anything you wanted to do.'

'Like what, frighten her off? Please leave my Daddy alone?'

'No, but you do know her sister, don't you, Deirdre?'

'Yes, Deirdre O'Donnell, she was in college with me. God.'

'So there we are.'

'There we are all right. Are you shocked?'

'I'm a bit stunned, like you. I can't see my father-in-law in the role, but I think I'm mainly sorry for poor Grandmama. I thought that's what you'd feel most.'

'No. Mother will survive. She's very rarely living in the real world anyway. She seems a bit stoned to me a lot of the time. I wouldn't be surprised if that doctor has her on valium most of the time. That's why he's such a success with all that generation, he just prescribes it by the ton . . . takes the edge off life, that's his motto.'

'Yes, well, it looks as if your mother's going to need her supply.'

'Yes, but in a way why should she? I mean if it's been going on for years, nothing's going to change.'

'I suppose not. Check the mileage, will you, I'm turning in here for petrol.'

Anna got out the little leather covered book and wrote in 11878 under mileage, Tralee under place, and then sat with her pencil poised until she could fill in the remaining two columns, gallons and price.

*   *   *

'I'm not going to spend a month going in and out playing cat and mouse with them. I'm not going to do it,' Sheila said on Sunday evening. She had the dining-room table covered with books that she was marking for tomorrow's class.

'I suppose you could just be there, you know, if she needed you, that would be a help,' said Martin. He was doing the crossword while Sheila corrected her exercises.

'That's not the point. It's unforgiveable being drawn into other peoples' rows and scenes and disasters. I'll never forgive him for accosting me like that and forcing me to take sides and attitudes. People shouldn't drag you into their unhappinesses, it's not fair.' She looked very cross and bit on the end of her pencil in annoyance.

'No, stop being tolerant and forgiving, Martin. It's a fact. We never drag people into our marriage, now do we?'

'No,' said Martin thoughtfully. 'But then we're very lucky we don't have any problems in our marriage.'

'No,' said Sheila sharply, going back to the exercise books. She had resolved long ago that if she was going to be the breadwinner, she wasn't going to complain and ruin it all by being a martyr. The only thing that made the whole bloody business worthwhile was that Martin had no idea how tired she was and how much she hated going in to that school each day. She thought of Carmel for a moment, and a great wave of impatience flooded over her. Carmel could get up at any time she liked, she had nothing more pressing in her day than to decide which clothes she should send to the St Vincent de Paul. Carmel's children were married. Well, Bernadette was as good as married. They weren't pounding home with huge appetites for meals which had to be prepared and shopped for. Sheila tried to give the appearance of being in charge of the kitchen so that Martin's sons should not think him a sissy. They still said 'thanks, Mum' when they found their clean clothes in their bedrooms, though as often as not it was their father who had done them.

In a way Carmel had only herself to blame if she was miserable and wretched over all this business about Ruth O'Donnell. Carmel was a lady of leisure with too much time to think about the too little she had to do. Then with a jolt Sheila remembered that it was she and Martin and Dermot who were wretched. Carmel had been very cheerful, and was in fact busy organising a dinner party and smartening up her wardrobe. Not at all what this wronged wife would have been expected to do.

* * *

Ethel and David had people in to bridge on Sunday night. They always had what they called a curfew on Sunday nights, and every one had to have played the last card by eleven-thirty.

When the car had driven off and they were emptying the ashtrays, opening the windows and taking out the dirty glasses to the dishwasher, Ethel said: 'I have the most awful feeling, like doom, as if something dreadful is going to happen. Do you know that feeling?'

'Every day going into work, and it's always accurate,' said David.

'Don't be trivial, you love your work, and why wouldn't you? People fussing over you, fuss fuss fuss all day. No, I have a sense of foreboding and I can't think what's causing it.'

'Maybe you feel guilty about something,' David said.

'It's that kind of feeling, that sort of heavy feeling in the chest, but I've nothing to be guilty about.'

'I think it's the bank manager's bit of skirt. I honestly think that's what's making us all so uneasy. I feel a bit edgy myself.'

'But we've known about it for ages.'

'Yes, but the poor sad wife must have only just found out.'

Ethel stood looking at a plate of peanuts thoughtfully. Eventually she tipped them into the pedal bin. 'I'd only eat them,' she said as an explanation, 'and they're more fattening than large g's and t's. I suppose that is what's making us nervous. It's such a mad thing to do. Such a very men in white coats mad thing to do. Ask the woman to dinner and have a public scene.'

'She won't go of course,' said David.

'No, but the fact that poor Carmel actually asked her is so mad. That's what's upsetting. Who knows what she'll do next, walk down Grafton Street in her knickers?'

*   *   *

Deirdre O'Donnell had no trouble in getting the porter to give her a key to her sister's flat. She said that Ruth wanted her to post on some things.

She wandered around, luxuriating in being alone among someone else's possessions. Now you could look and stare and ponder to your heart's content. Everyone else in the block had their sittingrooms carefully draped and framed. They looked like the rooms in a doll's house from outside. But Ruth's sitting room was bare, it was in fact her studio, and what other people regarded as the master bedroom and decked with fitted cupboards and thick carpets, Ruth used as a secondary studio and office. The small spare bedroom was her bedsitting room; a sofa that turned into a bed sat neatly in its sofa role, and in the kitchen the saucepans sat shining in a row.

For an artist her sister was very neat, Deirdre

thought. Spinsterish she had once believed ... that was before she knew about the regular visits of Anna Murray's father. FATHER. A bank manager. Maybe she should go to him to authorise an overdraft. Seriously, that's not a bad idea at all.

On the mat there were a dozen envelopes. Some were obviously brochures or advertisements. Then she saw the letter in the neat round handwriting. She eased it out carefully. It might be full of terrible intimate things ... things that Ruth would not want her to have read. She must steam the envelope; she could stick it all back with glue if it really was too yucky and Ruth would get into a temper.

Dear Ruth,
    I don't know whether you remember me or not, but we met a couple of times with David and Ethel O'Connor and you also know my friend Sheila Healy who says you gave a wonderful lecture at her school. Anyway, we are great admirers of yours and so looking forward to your exhibition on October 8th.
    I'm going to try to steal you for that night to come to dinner with us. This is why I'm writing to you so far in advance; I am sure you will get many invitations nearer the time but I want to be first in with mine. We will have the O'Connors and the Healys as well, so you will be among friends.
    Please let me know soon if you can come. I'm one of these middle-aged fussy sort of women who spend ages getting things organised, not like you and your friends. I'm sure you can combine about three lives successfully, but I'll be setting and resetting the table for days before you come, and then I'll pretend it all happened of its own accord.

It will give us all a great deal of pleasure if you say yes, and I know Dermot my husband would be thrilled. He has bought three of your paintings for our home. I hope you will like the way we have had them hung. So looking forward to seeing you.

Yours cordially,
Carmel Murray

Poor old cow, thought Deirdre, probably something wrong with her glands. She must know about Ruthie, half the country does. I don't think there's anything for old Dermot to get his knickers in a twist about, but I'd better ring her just in case.

Because Deirdre O'Donnell was essentially a frugal person she saw no reason why she shouldn't make the call from Ruth's own telephone. After all, it was Ruth's romance. It was Ruth's fellow's wife who had gone off her head . . . why not let Ruth pay for the call?

*   *   *

The farmer's wife knocked on her door and said there was a telephone call from Dublin.

'Your sister said you mustn't get alarmed. She says there is no problem.'

Ruth got up. She had been lying on the bed over the covers, reading. It was very luxurious somehow to do that, like going to the pictures in the afternoon.

'Ruthie?'

'What's happened?'

'Nothing, I told the old dame that. Nothing. Listen, Romeo asked me to contact you . . . '

'I told you I didn't want any messages. *Any.*'

'I told him that, he said that his wife has gone off

54

her head, and she's written to you.'

'Oh no.'

'It's all right, she hasn't called you the whore of Babylon. She's inviting you to dinner actually, the night your exhibition opens.'

'She's WHAT?'

'Do you want me to read it to you? "Dear Ruth, I don't know whether you remember me or not" . . . '

'Stop, stop. Is this serious?'

'Yes, but there's no abuse in it. Honestly, it's all full of admiration.'

'Oh Lord. What does Dermot say?'

'He wants to get in touch with you about it. I told him to leave you alone, but he said . . . '

'And did he say that she knows?'

'Ruthie . . . of course she knows. What are you talking about? She must know.'

'Dermot always said she didn't, or that if it came into her head she put it out again.'

'You must be mad. Do you think you're invisible or something, Ruthie? The two of you go everywhere together.'

'But if she knows, what's she inviting me to dinner for?'

'Well, that's the point, that's what Lover Boy was so much in a tizz about.'

'What does he think?'

'I don't know. I suppose he thinks that she's gone over the top, poor old thing. Do you want me to read it to you?'

'Yes, I suppose you'd better. If I've got to ring Dermot about it I'd better know what she says.'

'Right: "I don't know whether you remember me" . . . '

'Hey, Deirdre. This must be costing you a fortune.'

'No, it's costing you a fortune . . . the wages of sin, you know.'

'Oh go on, read it.'

*   *   *

Carmel planned her week carefully. It was nice to have so many things to do, it reminded her of being young again, when every day was so full and there seemed to be no waiting about. She would have to choose the main course and the dessert too. That would take two mornings in the bookshop reading the recipes. She was going to have a facial twice a week . . . oh, over on the North side of the city where she wouldn't be known . . . she would take the bus. She was going to spend two mornings shopping for her shoes. She had the dress already; the very good black dress which she had bought when Anna was 21 five years ago. She had worn it that evening . . . the first time . . . that first time when she had discovered about Dermot and the other girl . . . the time she had got so upset. She had never worn it again. But this time she would wear it and it would look magnificent. She would be much thinner . . . she was going to lose a stone this month. Her hair would be much more attractive . . . that man in Grafton Street who had done Ethel's hair was going to put highlights in for her a week before the party. She had telephoned and asked him what would be the best time. She had even told him she was a middle-aged lady, not a dollybird. 'I like coiffing mature ladies,' he had said.

Coiffing. It had sounded vaguely suggestive.

And there were so many other things to do. Window cleaners to come in. That firm which came and shampooed your carpet in the house. And her notebook to fill in.

She had written down anything anyone said about successful entertaining, like that thing Ethel had mentioned about the prawn cocktails and the roast beef.

She remembered Anna once talking about a house she had visited. 'They had fresh flowers in the bathroom, Mother, in the bathroom!' That had been included in the notebook. She had read an interview with a famous hostess who had said that the whole secret of successful entertaining was to have plenty of highly-polished glass and thick damask napkins on the table. That was noted, beside the advice about having a lot of salts, peppers and butterdishes so that people didn't have to keep passing them from one end of the table to the other.

Happier than she had been for a long time and armed with a list of the better cookery books, she started off for Donnybrook. At the hall door she met Anna.

'Oh dear! Why didn't you let me know you were coming, dear? I'm just off,' she said, regretfully but firmly pulling the door behind her.

'Hey, that's very welcoming,' Anna said, surprised. 'I bring your only grandchildren to visit you and that's what we get shown . . . the door.'

'Hallo Cilian . . . hallo Orla . . . ', she waved at them through the window.

Cilian struggled with his harness. 'Grandmama, Grandmama,' he called.

'Ah look, he wants to come to you,' Anna said.

'I'm sorry, darling, Granny's got to go out. Hallo Orla, blow Granny a kiss.'

'You might just ask us in for a cup of coffee.' Anna sounded huffed. 'We drove all the way in from

Sandycove to see you.'

'Oh, I am sorry.' Carmel was on her way to the gate.

'But where are you going to, Mother?'

'I'm going out dear, I have things to do. Will you still be in town this afternoon? Bring them in then and we'll have afternoon tea. Wouldn't that be nice?'

'Yes, but Mother, I wanted to have a little chat . . .'

'Grand. We'll have a little chat this afternoon.'

She was gone. Walking purposefully off towards the main road and the good brisk invigorating stretch towards the shops.

Anna looked after her, bewildered. Normally Mother was almost pathetically grateful for a visit, and fussed and ran about like an overgrown puppy. Here she was, striding off with no explanation. She looked after her, and Mother, as if she felt her eyes, turned and waved before she went around the corner. It was funny how people looked much younger when they moved quickly. Mother didn't look bad at all in her navy jacket and her check skirt. She didn't look fifty or fifty-one or whatever she was. Sometimes when she sat in that chair looking out into the back garden she looked seventy. Poor Mother, wasn't Dad awful to be fooling around with a young girl? Ruth O'Donnell too . . . but James was wrong, it couldn't be sex . . . it was just the thrill of the thing, the illicit excitement. Dad in bed with a girl? It was hard enough to imagine Dad being in bed with Mother years ago, but now . . . these days . . . Dad was so old he wouldn't even be interested in it, would he? And suppose he was, who in their right mind would go to bed with Dad?

58

Anna shrugged and got back into the car.

'Wasted journey,' she said to the children, who set up a simultaneous squawk of disappointment.

*　　　*　　　*

'Private call, Mr Murray, will you take it here or . . .?'

'That's all right, put me through . . . '

He knew it was Ruth from the way she spoke. She had a way of saying 'private call' that was almost lascivious.

'Dermot, can you talk?'

'Go ahead.'

'In other words you can't.'

'Not yet.'

'I got a call from Deirdre.'

'So she told you the situation . . . '

'She read me the letter, it sounded as if she doesn't have a clue.'

'Yes, well that's what I've always been saying . . .'

Dermot Murray's secretary felt she had tortured him enough. 'Excuse me,' she murmured and left the room.

'So what will I do . . . ?'

'Listen, darling love, when are you coming back?'

'In ten days, two weeks . . . '

'I love you.'

'You're alone now presumably . . . '

'No I'm in the board room, and the board all agree. They love you too.'

She giggled. 'Dermot, what will I do, will I write and say I'm tied up?'

'It means a lot to her, it means a great great deal. She's so lively and happy since she thought of the party, you have no idea, it stops that deadness. When

59

I see her like this I can really imagine her living a life, a normal life of her own . . . '

'So what do you want . . . ?'

'Could you accept?'

'Say I'd love to, and then sort of opt out at the last moment?'

Dermot paused. 'Yes . . . and, well, maybe in the end, if you could come, could go to the dinner. Could you?'

'WHAT?'

'Well, it wouldn't mean all that much to you . . . to us. We have so much, and there you are, a brilliant young girl with your life before you and all that . . . '

'You can't seriously expect me to come into your house as a guest, and say how nice, how delicious, you must give me the recipe for that boiled cabbage.'

'Ruth, please.'

'No, no please about it, you're sick, that's what you are. I couldn't possibly do it. I wouldn't dream of doing it to another woman, go in triumphantly and sit down with a lot of people who are in the secret. It's monstrous!'

'You don't understand . . . '

'I don't like what I do understand. Why are you going along with it?'

Her voice was upset; the pips went.

'We can't talk on the phone, let me come to see you.'

'NO. I wanted to be alone. You set all this up as a trick didn't you . . . admit it.'

'I swear to God I didn't, I swear I only heard about it on Friday. I might never have heard if I hadn't met David in the club. I don't think she was going to tell me.'

'You mean you were going to come home and find

everyone there?'

'I don't know. I don't know.'

'But she must have known that I would have told you . . . she must have known that . . . '

'She doesn't *know* about you and me! I keep telling you!'

'Deirdre says that's lunacy . . . half of Dublin knows.'

'Deirdre doesn't know anything — anyway, Carmel never meets half of Dublin.'

'Oh God, I knew you couldn't let me have this time without spoiling it. I knew you'd have to do something to balls it up for me.'

'That is so unfair. I don't even know where you are. I won't talk to you again until you come back. I just wanted you to know what happened. If I hadn't told you, you'd have said I was being devious, wouldn't you? Well, wouldn't you?'

She softened. 'I know.'

'So if you could do one thing for me, just one. Write a note and say that you are away in the country, that the letter was forwarded to you, and that you'd love to come. Can you do that?'

'No, Dermot, I am not a puppet, I will not be manipulated into awful, sordid, cruel scenes like that. I will not do it.'

'Just say you'll come, accept, people are always accepting things they don't go to in the end. Accept, and when you come back you and I will talk, and then you'll do whatever you like . . . '

'And you won't steamroll me into doing what I don't want to do?'

'No, Ruth my love, I will not.'

'And if I write this hypocritical note saying yes, you really think this is for the best . . . ?'

'I do.'

'For all of us, for her and for me, as well as for you?'

He paused. 'Yes. Seriously I do. For her, because she can go on planning her party and it will make her, well, busy and active again, and that's what we want. We want her to have a life of her own.'

'And how will it help *me*, to accept?'

'Well, you can stop worrying about it. Once you've written a letter saying yes, then a decision is made. You can unmake it any time, but you don't have to dither.'

'And how will it help you?'

'Then I can see her absorbed in something, and that's a hell of a lot more positive than seeing her sitting staring out the window and wondering what the future has in store.'

'What does the future have in store?'

'It has you coming home to me soon. It has your exhibition and all *that* means . . . '

'I wish I didn't love you.'

'I'm very glad you do.'

'A ridiculous married bank manager, hundreds of years older than me, knowing nothing about painting . . . '

'I know, I know.' He sounded soothing. He was happy now; once Ruth got on to the groove of how unsuitable he was, he felt safe.

'I must be quite mad.'

'You are, you are. Very,' he said.

'I'll write the letter, but I won't go.'

'Good girl,' he said.

*　　　*　　　*

Dear Mrs Murray,

What a nice surprise to get your letter.

I didn't even think you'd remember that we had met. It's very nice of you to say such flattering things about my work and I am most grateful for your dinner invitation on the night of the exhibition.

I am writing this from Wales where I am spending a quiet holiday. (My post is forwarded to me, so that's how I got your letter.) I should be very happy to accept. I look forward to renewing my friendship with you, your husband and your other friends.

Sincerely,
Ruth O'Donnell

Carmel held the letter tightly in her hand after she'd read it. Relief flooded her face. She had been almost certain that Ruth O'Donnell would accept, but there had been the slight fear that she might ruin the whole plan. Now everything was all right. Everything was on target.

That night Dermot told her that she was looking very well, very healthy-looking. Carmel smiled, pleased. 'I've been walking a lot lately, I find it does me good.' That was true, she did walk and it did make her feel as if it were doing good. But she didn't tell him about the facial she had had — the second this week. The beautician had been giving her a rejuvenating mask. And she didn't tell him that she had now settled on veal with marsala for the main course, and pears baked in wine for the dessert.

She didn't tell him that she had got a letter that day from Ruth O'Donnell.

*　　*　　*

Bernadette and Anna had lunch together. Anna had a salad and a coffee; Bernadette had a huge lump of French bread and cheese, and drank a pint of Guinness.

'Only point in having lunch in a pub, really, having a pint,' she said.

Anna swallowed her disapproval. They had met to discuss what they should do about Mother and Dad, if anything. There was no point in beginning by criticising each other.

'Are you sure . . . it's not just gossip?'

'No, a lot of people know, apparently we're the last to know.'

'Well, that stands to reason,' Bernadette said logically, 'people aren't going to discuss our father's little peccadillos in company where we are sitting there listening.'

'Now, should we say anything?'

'What could we say? Do you mean ask Dad is it true?'

Anna thought. 'Yes, we could do that I suppose, and sort of say that we think it's dreadful and that it must come to an end.'

Bernadette pealed with laughter.

'Anna, you are marvellous, you're just like a dowager duchess. "I think, Father, this is quite dreadful. It must come to an end. Back to Mother. Quick quick. As you were."' She rocked with amusement at the thought of it. Anna did not rock at all.

'Why is that funny? What do *you* suggest?'

'I'm sorry, I shouldn't laugh. What *do* I suggest? I don't know. I suppose we could ask him does he intend to go off with Ruth and leave Mother, because that's the only thing we have a *right* to know really.

I mean, if he does, she'll crack up . . . '

'Yes,' Anna agreed. 'That's the point. He must be made to see that he can't do that to her.'

'He may want to do it, but he must realise that's what's going to happen, and I suppose he should be given the facts about how much he can rely on you and on me . . . to pick up the bits.'

'Well, he can't expect us to look after . . . '

'No, he probably doesn't expect anything . . . I think he should be put in the picture, that's all . . .'

Anna was surprised to see her younger sister being so firm. She always thought of Bernadette as a bit eejity, but she was being very crisp today.

'Well, Frank and I are thinking of going to Australia in the New Year . . . '

'To Australia, like Uncle Charlie? *He* didn't make a fortune.'

'That's not the point. There's a crafts co-operative we are interested in. It's not definite yet, but I don't want Mummy to be one of my reasons for going or staying . . . I mean I'll write home every week and all . . . but I don't want to go not knowing whether she'll end up in a mental ward or whether she'll be all right . . . '

'Yes . . . yes.' Anna felt left behind.

'And *you're* not really going to move in and look after her, are you, Anna, you've got your own life . . . Dad should be told this . . . just so that he knows the options.'

'Yes. But isn't it all a bit harsh . . . a bit final? Mightn't we be sort of taking too much for granted . . .'

"Yes, that's the point . . . it was you who said we must meet and discuss what to do. I think that's the only thing to do if we do anything, let him know just how far he can rely on us so that there's no misunderstanding.'

'Yes, well I don't know, maybe we should say nothing . . . Mother's probably better able to look after herself than we realise . . . '

'And you were saying that she actually seems more lively these days.'

'Yes, and she looks better, her skin looks less sort of muddy . . . and she's lost a bit of weight I think . . . '

'She always seems very cheerful when I call in or ring.'

'Yes . . . when you think how awful it was that time her nerves did get bad.'

'Oh years ago, when I was still at college?'

'Yes, it was awful, she used to go and see this psychiatrist and cry all the time . . . '

'What did they do with her, how did they cure her?'

'Oh Bernadette, you know psychiatrists, they don't do anything or cure anyone . . . they just listen and say yes, yes . . . or so I hear.'

'Why do people go on going to them then?'

'Who knows, I suppose the world's a bit short on people who will listen and say yes, yes . . . '

'But she did get better, she stopped crying and everything . . . '

'I told you, it works, all this yes yessing.'

'And we'll say nothing for the moment . . . '

'I think not, don't you?'

*   *   *

Joe arrived a week before the party. He telephoned one morning and said he was in town.

'Did I send you enough money?' Carmel sounded

anxious.

'Darling, you sent me too much money. How are you, Carmel, am I going to come and see you?'

'No, I'll come and see you. I don't want you coming here until the night . . . '

'Where will we go?'

'Let me see . . . I'll go into the hotel . . . We can have tea or coffee sent up, can't we?'

'Yeah, it's costing a fortune the hotel . . . I wonder are you putting too much money out on all this, Carmel? There might have been another way . . . '

'I have the money . . . I've always had money, that was never a problem . . . I'm so grateful to you for coming over, Joe, I'll never be able to thank you. I wish your friend had come too.'

'No, a job's a job. Henry understands . . . it would have messed things up if he'd come here. He says you're as mad as a coot but he wishes you luck.'

She laughed happily. 'Oh good, he's on our side. I'll come down to the hotel this afternoon. What room are you? I'll just slip along and get into the lift . . . '

'Oh Mrs M., you sound as if you're accustomed to this kind of racey life,' Joe laughed. He was pleased that Carmel was so cheerful, he had been afraid that it might be a very glum Carmel. A sort of doom-laden Lady Macbeth. This sounded a lot more jolly. He sat back in his bed and lit a cigarette. It was really the most extraordinary business.

*   *   *

'How nice of you to call, Ethel. No, I'm fine . . . and you? Good. And David? Great. Oh, what a pity, no, I'm just off out as a matter of fact. Yes it is a long time, isn't it? But never mind, we'll see you next week, won't we? The eighth. Oh good, good. No, not a thing, thank you, no, no, it's all under control. But very nice of you to think of it, Ethel . . . What? Oh yes, everyone's coming . . . but it's only a small gathering, heavens, compared to all the ones you go to. Yes, that nice Ruth O'Donnell — I had such a sweet letter from her, Wales is where she was. She's looking forward to seeing you all again, she said. Was there anything else, Ethel? I'm in a bit of a rush. Right, see you both then, love to David. Bye.'

*　　　*　　　*

'Yes, Aunt Sheila, I'm on my own. I've plenty of time to talk. She seems in great form to me, very perky. And looking very well, I think she looks better now than I've seen her looking for a long time . . . good, yes I thought I wasn't imagining it. No, of course I don't mind you talking frankly. I mean I know you're her oldest friend, for heaven's sake. No, honestly Aunt Sheila I'm telling you the truth, I haven't noticed anything odd about Mother recently . . . she's in very good form . . . Yes, well she doesn't have much time for me either. No, I'm not actually sure what she *is* doing but whatever little things they are seem to keep her occupied. The way I look at it, isn't she far better this way all cheerful and mysterious than she was the time she got upset and her nerves were bad? Do you remember she sat there all day and we all found it a terrible drag to talk to her . . . she had no interest in anyone.'

*　　　*　　　*

Anna said to James: 'You know that friend of Mother's, the one we call Aunt Sheila who went back to teaching, remember? She was on the phone whinging and whining and says that she thinks Mother's behaving oddly. How oddly, I ask, and she can't explain. Apparently Mother is too cheerful. Did you ever?'

'Poor Grandmama,' said James, 'it's bad if she's gloomy, it's bad if she's cheerful. She can't win.'

* * *

'You look a million dollars . . . you're *not* an old hag . . . you're smashing.' Joe was full of admiration.

'I had a make-up lesson . . . you know the kind of thing the womens' magazines advise you to do if your husband's unfaithful. "Is your make-up old-fashioned," they ask, and recommend you to try out the new shades . . . '

They both laughed, and she looked at him carefully and nodded with approval.

'You look well, Joe, really well. I'm different, I'm just painted up a bit, that's why I appear to be ok, but you're really great . . . you look like a boy.'

'An old boy,' Joe laughed. 'Oh, a very old boy . . . I'll be forty-five soon. That's not a boy these days!'

'You look still in your thirties and you look terrific . . . '

Joe was pleased that her admiration was genuine. 'Do you know what I did for us, I went out to that supermarket up in Baggot Street . . . Lord has the place all changed . . . and I got us a bottle of fizz, on me. I decided that if we're going to do this mad thing we'll celebrate it in style.'

'Do you think we should wait until it's done?'

Carmel was unwilling to celebrate yet.

'Hell no, if we say we'll do it, then it will be done.' He opened the bottle with a practised hand and poured into the tooth mugs. 'Of course, I still think you're as daft as a brush.'

'Why? To get what I want? To try and get what I want?'

'No.' He raised his glass to her. 'Cheers, good luck. No, that's not daft. To want it is daft.'

'Cheers,' she said, raising her glass. 'Ninety calories for four fluid ounces . . . how many in this glass?'

'I think we could say bang goes 180 calories there.'

They laughed like old times.

*　　　*　　　*

'We've done nothing but fight since you came back. It's the last thing on God's earth that I want to do.'

'We haven't been fighting,' Ruth said wearily. 'I keep asking one question and you keep asking it back. I keep saying why do I have to go to this dinner and you keep saying why not. It's not so much a fight, it's a cul-de-sac.'

Dermot sighed. 'I keep telling you that we're buying time, that's all it is . . . buying peace of mind and opportunities . . . all of these things we want, and we can get them if you just come to the house and behave nice and naturally and let everybody tell you how wonderful you are for one evening. I know, I know, you don't want to, but it doesn't seem too hard a thing to me.'

She got up and walked around her kitchen. 'And it seems amazing to me that you don't see how hard it is to do. To go and talk to her, and to smile . . . and eat the food she's been slaving over, and go to the lavatory in your bathroom, and leave my coat on your bed, your marriage bed . . . really, Dermot . . .'

'If I've told you once there are single beds I've told you twenty times . . . this time you'll be able to see for yourself.'

'It's almost as if you felt like a big man, having us both there . . .'

'Christ, God, if you knew how that is not true . . . I'll feel nervous and uneasy and anxious . . . and I'll feel a cheat and a deceiver. Do you think I want to draw all that on myself?'

'Please, Dermot . . . '

'Please, Ruth, please . . . I never asked you anything like this before and I swear I'll never ask you again.'

'Oh, for all I know it could become a weekly affair, maybe I'll be invited to move in . . . put a third bed in the room.'

'Don't be coarse.'

'Isn't it bad enough to deceive her without rubbing her nose in it?'

'Ruth, I love you, don't you know?'

'I think you do, but it's like believing in God — sometimes it's very difficult to remember why you ever did . . . '

* * *

'Aren't you having even numbers, Mother? I thought you were asking me once about how to seat eight at a table.'

It was the day before the party. Anna had dropped in to check up on Mother. Bernadette was right, Mother had never looked better, slimmer and with colour in her cheeks, or could that possibly be a blusher? And what smart shoes! Mother said she had bought them for tomorrow and she was running them in. They were super, they cost about twice as much as Anna would have paid for a pair of shoes and ten times what she thought Mother would have paid.

'No, just seven ... I suppose I did think of getting an extra man, but people say that it's very old-fashioned nowadays making up the numbers. Ethel says that more dinners have been ruined by people struggling to make the sexes equal ... '

'Oh yes ... I quite agree, really dreary men being dragged in, there are more really dreary men than dreary women around, I always think ... '

'So do I, but maybe we're prejudiced!' Mother laughed, and Anna laughed too. Mother was fine, what was all the fuss about? In order to let Mother think she was interested in the famous dinner, she asked brightly, 'Who's coming then, Mother? Aunt Sheila and Uncle Martin I suppose ...'

'Yes, and Ethel and David ... and Ruth O'Donnell, that nice young artist.'

Anna dropped her handbag.

'Who ...?'

'Oh, you must know her, the painting in the hall, and this one. And the one on the stairs. Ruth O'Donnell ... her exhibition opens tomorrow, and we're all going to it and then coming back here for dinner.'

*   *   *

Bernadette wasn't in, but Anna told the whole thing to Frank and had a glass of parsnip wine to restore her.

'Are there bits of parsnip in it?' she asked suspiciously.

'No, it's all fermented, it's all we have,' Frank said ungraciously.

Anna told the whole story, interspersed with explanations of how her heart had nearly stopped and she hadn't known what to say, to think, to do. Frank listened blankly.

'Isn't she a fifteen-carat bitch,' Anna said in the end.

'Your mother?' Frank asked, puzzled.

'No, the woman. Ruth O'Donnell. Isn't she a smug self-satisfied little bitch? It's not enough for her to have her own exhibition which half the country seems to be going to, it's not enough for her to have poor Dad like a little lap poodle running after her . . . she has to get him to get Mother to ask her to a dinner party and make a public humiliation of her in front of all Mother's friends.'

Frank looked unmoved.

'Well, isn't it appalling,' she snapped.

He shrugged. 'To me there are two ways of looking at it, and both of them are from your Ma's point of view. Either she knows, in which case she knows what she's doing, or she doesn't know, in which case nobody's about to announce it to her over the soup, so either way *she's* all right.'

Anna didn't like the way Frank had emphasised the word *she*. If he meant that Mother was all right, who wasn't? Could it be Anna, sharp and shrill and getting into a tizz? She drained her parsnip wine and left.

* * *

'For God's sake, stay out of it,' James said. 'Don't

ring all those fearful old women up. Let it go its own way. You'll hear soon enough if something disastrous happens.'

'But they're my own mother and father, James. It's not as if they were just neighbours. You have to care about your own mother and father.'

'Your own daughter and son seem to be yelling for you in the kitchen,' he said.

She flounced out. James came out after her and gave her a kiss. She smiled and felt better. 'That's soppy,' said Cilian and they all laughed.

*　　　*　　　*

RTE rang and asked if Ruth would go on the Day by Day programme. She said she would call them back.

'Should I?' she asked Dermot.

'Definitely,' he said. 'Absolutely. Go straight out.'

Thank God, he thought, at least that will take her mind off Carmel and the dinner. This time tomorrow it would all be over, he told himself. This time tomorrow he would sit down and take stock of his life. He had all the information that anyone could ever gather about early retirement plans ... or he could ask for a transfer.

Ruth had often said she would like to live out of Dublin, but of course in a small place it wouldn't be acceptable ... anyway, no point in thinking about all that now; the main thing was that Carmel was quite capable of living a life of her own now ... might even get herself a job like her friend Sheila. That was something that could be suggested, not by him, of course ... Oh God, if she only knew how he wanted her to be happy, he didn't want to hurt her, or betray her, he just wanted her to have her own life.

'Your wife on the line, Mr Murray.'

He jumped physically. 'What? What?'

'Shall I put her through?'

'Of course . . . '

Carmel never rang him at the bank; what could have happened?

'Hallo, Dermot, I'm awfully sorry for bothering you, were you in the middle of someone's bank account?'

'No of course not. What is it, Carmel?'

'Do you remember Joe Daly?'

'What? Who?'

'I was asking you did you remember Joe Daly, he used to write for the paper here, then he went off to London . . . remember?'

'Vaguely, I think. Why?'

'Well, I met him quite by chance today, and he's been doing interviews with Ruth O'Donnell, he knows her quite well it turns out . . . anyway I thought I'd ask him tonight, isn't that a good idea?'

'Joe who?'

'Daly, do you remember, a mousey little man . . . we knew him ages ago before we were married.'

'Oh he's our age . . . right, whatever you say. If you think he's nice, then do. Whatever you like, dear. Will he fit in with everyone else?'

'Yes, I think so, but I wanted to check.'

'Sure, sure, ask him, ask him.'

Thank God, he thought, thank God, a mousey little failed journalist to talk about things that none of them were tied up in. There was a God in heaven, the night might not be so dreadful after all. He was about to dial Ruth when he realised she was probably on her way to the studio.

'Can you record "Day by Day", please, on the

machine over there,' he said to Miss O'Neill. 'There's going to be an item on banking I'd like to hear later.' He watched as she put on the cassette, checked her watch and set the radio tape recorder to begin at eleven.

*　　*　　*

Joe rang her at noon on the day of the party.

'Can I come up now?' he asked.

'Be very careful, look like a tradesman,' she said.

'That's not hard,' he said.

She looked around the house. It was perfect. There were flowers in the bathroom, lovely dahlias and chrysanthemums, all in dark reds, they looked great with the pink soaps and pink towels. The bedroom where they were going to leave their coats was magnificent, with the two thick Kilkenny Design bedspreads freshly cleaned. The kitchen had flowers in it too, orange dahlias and rust chrysanthemums; she had bought teatowels just in that colour. Really, it was such fun showing off. She didn't know why she hadn't done it ages ago.

*　　*　　*

He came in very quickly. She looked left and right, but the houses weren't near enough for anyone to see.

'Come in and tell me everything,' she said.

'It's worked . . . so far.'

She poured a coffee for him.

'Won't it spoil the beautiful kitchen?' he teased.

'I have five hours to tidy it up,' she laughed.

'So, I'll tell you from the start. I arrived at her flat,

your man was in there, I could hear his voice. They were arguing . . . '

'What about?' Carmel was interested.

'I couldn't hear. Anyway, I waited, I went down to the courtyard place. I sat on the wall and waited, he left in an hour. I pressed her bell. I told her who I was, that I had an interest in a gallery in London, that I didn't want to set up huge business meetings and press her in the week of her exhibition but I was very interested in seeing whether it was the kind of thing we could bring to London.'

'Did she ask why you were at the door?'

'Yes. I said I'd looked her up in the phone book . . . she thought that was very enterprising . . . '

'It is,' laughed Carmel. 'Nobody ever thinks of it.'

'Anyway I told her I was staying at the hotel but that if she liked we could talk now. She laughed and said why not now, and let me in . . . '

'And . . . ?'

'And it's very nice, all done up as a studio, not a love nest at all . . . hardly any comfort, nothing like this . . .' He looked around the smart kitchen and through the open door into the dining room with its dark polished wood. 'So we had a long talk, all about her work. She showed me what she was doing, showing, we went through the catalogue. I explained what I could do . . . Jesus, if you'd heard the way I dropped the names of galleries and people in London — I even impressed myself. I promised nothing. I said I'd act as a middleman. I even sent myself up a bit and said I saw myself as a Mister Fixit . . . she liked that and she laughed a lot . . . '

'Yes,' said Carmel before he could say it. 'I know, I know, I've heard. She's very nice. Go on.'

'Yes, well. I think I played it well. I must have.

When I was leaving I said that we must keep in touch, that I could be here for a week and perhaps she would like to have a lunch one day. She said that would be nice, and I said the next day and we picked the place you said . . . I said I'd heard it was good.'

'Was it?' asked Carmel with interest.

'It was and so it should be, it cost you an arm and a leg. I kept the receipt for you . . . '

'Joe, I don't need receipts.'

'I know, but it is *astronomical.*'

'Was it the right place . . . ?'

'Yes, we sat on and on. She doesn't drink much but they kept bringing pots of coffee . . . nobody rushed us . . . it was very relaxed and we broadened the conversation . . . she told me about how she began and how this nun at the school she went to had great faith in her even when her parents didn't really believe she had talent.'

Joe paused. 'I kept leaning heavily on the notion that I was just passing through, not a permanent fixture. She was quite anxious to talk actually, I don't need much congratulation.'

'So she did tell you . . .

'Yes, I sort of squeezed it out of her bit by bit . . . not with crude questions like, "Why isn't a girl like you married?" More about Dublin being full of gossip and disapproval . . . I told her I'd never be able to live here nowadays because of my own life. She said no, it wasn't too bad . . . things had changed, but people did let others go their own way. I argued that with her, and then she had to get down to specifics. She had a false start, then she said she didn't want to be unburdening her whole life story to a total stranger.

'I said that total strangers were the only people you could possibly unburden things to. They passed like ships in the night. Sometimes it happened that you got a bit of advice from a passing ship but even if you didn't, what the hell, the ship had passed on . . . it wasn't hanging around embarrassing you every time you saw it . . . '

'And?'

'And she told me . . . she told me about her married man.'

'Was it anything like the truth? I mean, did she describe things the way things are?'

'Very like the way you told me. She met him when she was doing a job for the bank. He had taken her out to lunch, she had been lonely, he had understood . . . her father had died recently. Her mother was dead years ago. The married man was very sympathetic.'

'I'm sure,' said Carmel.

'They met a lot and he was so interested in her work and so encouraging . . . and he believed in her — and the reason she liked him so much . . . '

'Yes . . . ?' Carmel leaned forward.

'He didn't want to hurt people or do people down. He never wanted her to score over other people. He wanted her to be content in herself and with her work . . . she liked that most about him.'

Joe paused. 'So I put it to her that he must have a bit of the louse in him to maintain two ménages, he must be a bit of a crud to have it both ways . . . you know, not disturbing his own lifestyle . . . '

'What did she say?'

'She thought not, she thought he was a victim of circumstances. His wife hadn't been well, she had been — sorry, Carmel — the phrase she used was "suffering from her nerves" . . . '

'Fine, fine,' said Carmel.

'Then I talked about Henry a bit, I didn't want her to think that she was confiding too much, you know ... people turn against people when they tell them too much.'

'Yes I know,' Carmel agreed.

'So anyway it went on from there ... could she guide me around Dublin a bit? We had lunch at the National Gallery ... we went in and out of the place that's giving her the exhibition, we went — oh, God knows where ... I kept her occupied during the days, and I faded out a bit at night because I knew she'd be meeting your man after work. On Wednesday she asked me would I like to meet him. I said no.'

'Wednesday,' Carmel said softly to herself.

'Yes. I said no way did I want to get involved in peoples' private lives. That was the night she told me that she had been invited here and she was worried sick, she couldn't think why ... She said she didn't want to come and hurt you.'

'No. No, indeed,' said Carmel.

'So she said she didn't know how to get out of it, the Man wouldn't hear of her refusing. I said the married man wanted to get a kick out of seeing you both together. She went quite white over it all ... "He wouldn't want that," she said. "I don't know, it gives some fellows a real charge," I said, "seeing the two women there and knowing they've screwed both of them."'

'Really?' Carmel said.

Joe laughed. 'That's what she said too. Anyway, it upset her. And she said he wasn't like that. Well then, he shouldn't force you to come to the dinner, I said. It's being a real voyeur, isn't it, having the both of you there?'

Joe paused for a gulp of his coffee.

'Then I said, "I wouldn't be surprised if he forced the wife to ask you to dinner, after all why would the wife ask you? If she doesn't know about you and him it's an odd thing she should suddenly decide to pick you of all the people in Dublin and if she *does* know it's even odder." She said that's what she'd been thinking herself. She's just an ordinary woman you know, Carmel, just an ordinary female with a slow brain ticking through and working things out ... she's no Mata Hari.'

'I know,' said Carmel.

'So I said then, and the others are his friends really, maybe they're all in on it, they know about you and him, don't they?' Joe leaned over. 'So that was part one over, she really believed he was setting her up, she was so convinced. I don't know what kind of an evening they had that night, but it didn't last long. He was out of there in an hour.'

'Yes, he was home very bad-tempered and very early on Wednesday,' Carmel said, smiling.

'So Thursday I ring her and say come on, I'll buy you lunch and no gloomy chat, because isn't it a small world, I've just run into my old friends the Murrays and ha ha isn't Dublin a village? I now know who the mystery bank manager is, it's Dermot Murray. I didn't know he knew you ... She's amazed.

'"Oho," I say, "can't keep a secret in this town. No, really, isn't it a scream, I knew brother Charlie years ago, long before he went to Australia or anything, and I remember Carmel, and Carmel was walking out with Dermot Murray, a lowly bank clerk then ..." Oh she's all upset, she can't believe it, it's too much. I say stop all that fussing and fretting, I'll buy you a big lunch. I keep saying it's a scream ... '

Carmel smiled.

'I arrive and collect her. She's been crying, she's so ashamed, she wouldn't have dreamed of telling me all those intimate things if there was a chance I'd have known anyone . . . but I was a stranger in town and outside, someone who went away years ago . . . I kept laughing, the odds against it must be millions to one, forget it, anyway wasn't it all for the best? Because now that I knew that it was Carmel and Dermot I could say definitely that they weren't the kind of people who would be involved in anything sordid. Everyone had spoken very well of Dermot, and poor Carmel had always been very nice.'

'Poor Carmel,' Carmel said, smiling still.

'You asked me to play it for all I could,' Joe said.

'I know. Go on.'

'It took a lot of coaxing to get her back where she was. I reminded her of all the indiscretions I had told her, about being gay, about Henry. I told her that nobody in Ireland knew that about me, that we each knew secrets about the other. We shook hands over lunch. I felt a real shit.'

'Joe, go on.'

'She left more cheerful. I rang her yesterday morning and asked could I come by for coffee. I told her that I had heard at the hotel a man talking to a friend. I described David perfectly . . . he's not hard to describe from what you told me.'

'There's only one David,' said Carmel.

'Yes, well she identified him, and oh I wove a long tale. It could have been something else entirely, but it did sound as if it could have been Dermot he was talking about . . . I kept pretending that it might have been imagination but she saw it wasn't. She knew that if I had heard him talking like that it must be Dermot, and Dermot must indeed have told David that she was coming to the party and wasn't it all very risqué.'

Joe looked at Carmel. 'She cried a lot, she cried and cried. I felt very sorry for her.'

'I cried a lot. I cried for four months the first time, the time he went off with that Sophie.'

'But she has nobody to comfort her.'

'I had nobody to comfort me.'

'You had a psychiatrist.'

'Great help.'

'He cured you, didn't he?'

'No he didn't, he asked me to ask myself was my marriage with Dermot so important that I should save it at all costs. What the hell does he know about marriage and importance, and all costs? What else is there for me but to be married to Dermot? There *is* nothing else. It's not a choice between this and something else, it's this or nothing.'

'You're fine, you could live on your own. You don't need him. I can't see what you want him around for. He hasn't been any good to you for years, he hasn't been kind or a friend. You haven't wanted any of the things he wanted. Why didn't you let him go then, or indeed now?'

'You don't understand. Its different for ... er ... Gays, it's not the same.'

'Hell, it's not the same, of course it's not the same. I love Henry, Henry loves me. One day one of us will stop loving the other. Hopefully we'll split and go our own ways ... but the worst is to stay together bitching.'

'But your world, it's so different ... so totally different ... I couldn't do that.'

'Well you didn't. And you've won.'

'I have, haven't I?'

'Yes . . . it's all fixed up. I told her this morning that I'd been asked here, that I'd be here for moral support if she wanted to come. She said no, she didn't want to make a fool of herself in front of everyone. She'll tell you tonight at the exhibition that she can't come after all. She says she'll do it gently, she knows you are just as much a pawn as she is . . .'

'Good, good.'

'And she's not going to tell him at all. She's going to leave him stew, let him think what he likes.'

'Suppose he runs after her, suppose he won't let her go?'

'I think she'll make it clear to him. Anyway, she's already set up some other friends to go out with. She says she's sorry for you because you're a timid sort of person and you'd been planning this for a month . . . she's afraid that the whole thing will be a damp squib . . .'

'That's very nice of her.'

'It is actually, Carmel, she's a very nice person.'

'So you keep saying, but I'm a very nice person. I'm an extremely nice person, and very few people ever realise that.'

'I realise it. I've always realised it,' Joe said.

'Yes,' Carmel said.

'I'd have done this for no money, you were always good to me.'

'I sent you money because I have it, you don't. It seemed only fair that your week should be subsidised . . .'

'You were always a brick, Carmel. Always. I'd have had no life if it weren't for you.'

There was a silence. In the gleaming kitchen they sat and remembered the other kitchen, the kitchen where Carmel's brother Charlie and Joe had stood scarlet-faced in front of Carmel's father. Words that had never been used in that house were used that evening. Threats of ruin were made. Joe would be prosecuted, he would spend years and years in goal, the whole world would know about his unnatural habits, his vile seduction of innocent schoolboys ... an act so shameful not even the animal kingdom would tolerate it, and Charlie might grow up warped as a result. Joe's father who worked as the gardener would be sacked, and the man would never work again. He would be informed this night of his son's activities.

It was then that Carmel had found her voice. She was five years older than Charlie, she was twenty-two. She had been a quiet girl, her father had not even noticed her in the kitchen so great had been his rage.

'It was Charlie's fault, Dad,' she had said in a level voice. 'Charlie's been queer for two years. He's had relationships with a lot of boys, I can tell you their names.' There had been a silence which seemed to last for an hour. 'I don't like unfairness. Joe Daly has done nothing that Charlie didn't encourage. Why should his father be sacked, why should he be disgraced, why should Charlie get away with it, Dad, because Mr Daly is a gardener and you're a Company Director?'

It was unanswerable.

Charlie went to Australia shortly afterwards. Mr Daly was never told, and Joe Daly got a little assistance from Charlie's father indirectly, so that he could go to a technical school and do English and commerce and book-keeping. During that time he wrote the odd article for evening papers, and Carmel had seen him casually around Dublin. He had sent her a wedding present when she married Dermot two years after the distressing events in the kitchen. It was a beautiful cut glass vase, nicer than anything she had got from any of her father's friends, or any of Dermot's side. It would be on the dining-table tonight, with late summer roses in it.

* * *

'So will I leave you to rest and think over it all?' Joe said.

'I *wish* you thought I'd done the right thing,' she said.

'You know what I think. I think you should have given him away. I really do. There are other lives.'

'Not for fifty-year-old women there aren't.'

'I know what you mean, but there are. Anyway, there you go.'

'Why are you so fed up with me?'

'Carmel, I'm not fed up with you. I owed you, I'd do anything for you anytime, I told you that and I meant it. You asked me one favour. You've paid me handsomely for it. I've done it, but I don't have to approve of it.'

'Oh, Joe, I thought you'd understand.'

'You see, it's the total reverse of all that happened, years ago. Then you did something brave just . . . well . . . just so that the right thing should be done . . .'

'But this is the right thing! She's young, she'll find somebody else, a proper person, not a married man . . . not somebody else's husband . . .'

'No, you see this time you've arranged it so that the truth is hidden, lost . . . She thinks that Dermot is setting her up, she thinks he's having a laugh at her, that he wanted her to come to the party as some kind of macho thing. Dermot thinks that she's let him

86

down, promised to go through with it and then thrown him over unexpectedly. Neither believes that the other is actually honest.'

Carmel stood up. 'I know it's complicated. That psychiatrist said to me, you know, the first time, that there's no such thing as absolute right and absolute wrong. He also said that we can't control other peoples' lives, we must only take responsibility for our own. I decided what I wanted to do with mine, and I did it. That's the way I see it. I don't see it as meddling or playing God or anything.'

Joe stood up too. 'No, whatever else it is, I don't think it's playing God,' he said.

And he slipped quietly out of the house, making sure that he wasn't observed, because he wasn't meant to be a great friend of Carmel's, he was only a casual friend whom they had met luckily again, and his last job was to make sure that the dinner party was great fun.

FLAT IN RINGSEND

11

They said you should get the evening papers at lunch-time and as soon as you got a smell of a flat that would suit you were to rush out and sit on the step at the head of the queue. You shouldn't take any notice of the words 'After six o'clock'. If you got there at six o'clock and the ad had sounded any way reasonable then you'd find a line trailing down the road. Finding a good flat in Dublin at a price you could afford was like finding gold in the gold rush.

The other way was by personal contact; if you knew someone who knew someone who was leaving a place that often worked. But if you had only just arrived in Dublin there was no chance of any personal contact, nobody to tell you that their bedsit would be vacant at the end of the month. No, it was a matter of staying in a hostel and searching.

Jo had been to Dublin a dozen times when she was a child; she had been up for a match, or for a school outing, or the time that Da was in the Chest Hospital and everyone had been crying in case he wouldn't get better. Most of her friends had been up to Dublin much more often; they talked about places they had gone to in a familiar way, and assumed that she knew what they were talking about.

'You *must* know the Dandelion Market. Let me see, you come out of the Zhivago and you go in a straight line to your right, keep going and you pass O'Donoghues and the whole of Stephen's Green, and you don't turn right down Grafton Street. Now do you know where it is?'

After so much effort explaining things to her, Jo said she did. Jo was always anxious to please other people, and she felt that she only annoyed them by not knowing what they were talking about. But Dublin was a very big blank spot. She really felt she was stepping into the unknown when she got on the train to go and work there. She didn't ask herself why she was going in the first place. It had been assumed by everyone that she would go. Who would stay in a one-horse town, the back of beyonds, the end of the world, the sticks, this dead-and-alive place? That's all she had heard for years. At school they were all going to get out, escape, see some life, get some living in, have a real kind of existence, and some of the others in her class had gone as far as Ennis or Limerick, often to stay with cousins. A few had gone to England, where an elder sister or an aunt would see them settled in. But out of Jo's year none of them were going to Dublin. Jo's family must have been the only one in the place who didn't have relations in Glasnevin or Dundrum. She was heading off on her own.

There had been a lot of jokes about her going to work in the Post Office. There'd be no trouble in getting a stamp to write a letter home; what's more, there'd be no excuse if she didn't. She could sneak the odd phone call too, which would be fine, but they didn't have a phone at home. Maybe she could send a ten-page telegram if she needed to say anything in a hurry. They assumed that she would know the whole business of the high and the mighty in

Dublin the way Miss Hayes knew everyone's business from the post office at home. People said that she'd find it very easy to get to know people, there was nowhere like a post office for making friends, it was the centre of everything.

She knew she wouldn't be working in the GPO, but whenever she thought of herself in Dublin it was in the middle of the General Post Office chatting up all the people as they came in, knowing every single person who came to buy stamps or collect the children's allowances. She imagined herself living somewhere nearby, maybe over Clery's or on the corner of O'Connell Bridge so that she could look at the Liffey from her bedroom.

She had never expected the miles and miles of streets where nobody knew anyone, the endless bus journeys, the having to get up two hours before she was meant to be at work in case she got lost or the bus was cancelled. 'Not much time for a social life,' she wrote home. 'I'm so exhausted when I get back to the hostel I just go to bed and fall asleep.'

Jo's mother thought that it would be great altogether if she stayed permanently in the hostel. It was run by nuns, and she could come to no harm. Her father said that he hoped they kept the place warm; nuns were notorious for freezing everyone else to death just because they wore thermal underwear. Jo's sisters who worked in the hotel as waitresses said she must be off her head to have stayed a whole week in a hostel; her brother who worked in the Creamery said he was sorry she didn't have a flat, it would be somewhere to stay whenever he went to Dublin; her brother who worked in the garage said that Jo would have been better off to stay where she was — what would she get in Dublin only discontented, and she'd end up like that O'Hara girl, neither one thing nor the other, happy neither in Dublin nor at home. It had to be said that he had fancied the O'Hara girl for a long time, and it was a great irritation to him that she wouldn't settle down and be like a normal woman.

But Jo didn't know that they were all thinking about her and discussing her, as she answered the advertisement for the flat in Ringsend. It said *'Own room, own television, share kitchen, bathroom'*. It was very near her post office and seemed too good to be true. Please, St Jude, please. May it be nice, may they like me, may it not be too dear.

There wasn't a queue for this one because it wasn't so much 'Flat to Let', more 'Third Girl Wanted'. The fact that it had said 'Own Television' made Jo wonder whether it might be in too high a class for her, but the house did not look any way overpowering. An ordinary red-bricked terraced house with a basement. Her father had warned her against basements; they were full of damp, he said, but then her father had a bad chest and saw damp everywhere. But the flat was not in the basement, it was upstairs. And a cheerful-looking girl with a college scarf, obviously a failed applicant, was coming down the stairs.

'Desperate place,' she said to Jo, 'They're both awful. Common as dirt.'

'Oh,' said Jo and went on climbing.

'Hallo,' said the girl with 'Nessa' printed on her tee-shirt.

'God, did you see that toffee-nosed bitch going out? I can't stand that kind, I can't stand them . . . '

'What did she do?' asked Jo.

'Do? She didn't have to *do* anything. She just poked around and wrinkled her lip and sort of giggled and then said "Is this it?" in a real Foxrock accent.

"Oh dear, oh dear." Stupid old cow, we wouldn't have had her in here if we were starving and needed her to buy us a crust, would we, Pauline?'

Pauline had a pyschedelic shirt on; it almost hurt the eyes but was only marginally brighter than her hair. Pauline was a punk, Jo noted with amazement. She had seen some of them on O'Connell Street, but hadn't met one close up to talk to.

'No, stupid old bore. She was such a bore. She'd have bored us to death, years later our bodies would have been found here and the verdict would have been death by boredom . . . '

Jo laughed. It was such a wild thought to think of all that pink hair lying on the floor dead because it hadn't been able to stand the tones of the flat-mate. 'I'm Jo, I work in the post office and I rang . . .' Nessa said they were just about to have a mug of tea. She produced three mugs; one had 'Nessa' and one had 'Pauline' and the other one had 'Other' written on it. 'We'll get your name put on if you come to stay,' she said generously.

Nessa worked in CIE, and Pauline worked in a big firm nearby. They had got the flat three months ago and Nessa's sister had had the third room, but now she was getting married very quickly, very quickly indeed, and so the room was empty. They explained the cost, they showed her the geyser for having a bath and they showed her the press in the kitchen, each shelf with a name on it, Nessa, Pauline and Maura.

'Maura's name will go, and we'll paint in yours if you come to stay,' Nessa said again reassuringly.

'You've no sitting room,' Jo said.

'No, we did it in three bed-sits,' said Nessa.

'Makes much more sense,' said Pauline.

'What's the point of a sitting-room?' asked Nessa.

'I mean, who'd sit in it?' asked Pauline.

'And we've got two chairs in our own rooms,' Nessa said proudly.

'And each of us has our own telly,' said Pauline happily.

That was the point that Jo wanted to discuss.

'Yes, you didn't say how much that costs. Is there a rental?'

Nessa's big happy face spread into a grin. 'No, that's the real perk. You see, Maura's Steve, well my brother-in-law as he now is, I hope, my brother-in-law Steve worked in the business and he was able to get us tellys for a song.'

'So you bought them outright, did you?' Jo was enthralled.

'Bought in a manner of speaking,' Pauline said. 'Accepted them outright.'

'Yeah, it was his way of saying thank you, his way of paying the rent . . . in a manner of speaking,' Nessa said.

'But did he stay here too?'

'He was Maura's boy-friend. He stayed most of the time.'

'Oh ' said Jo. There was a silence.

'Well?' Nessa said accusingly. 'If you've anything to say, you should say it now.'

'I suppose I was wondering did he not get in everyone's way. I mean, if a fourth person was staying in the flat was it fair on the others?'

'Why do you think we organised it all into bedsits?' Pauline asked. 'Means we can all do what we like when we like, not trampling on other people. Right?'

'Right,' Nessa said.

'Right,' Jo said, doubtfully.

'So what do you think,' Nessa asked Pauline. 'I think Jo would be OK if she wants to come, do you?'

'Yeah, sure, I think she'd be fine if she'd like it here,' said Pauline.

'Thank you', said Jo, blushing a bit.

'Is there anything else you'd like to ask? I think we've covered everything. There's a phone with a coin-box in the hall downstairs. There's three nurses in the flat below, but they don't take any messages for us so we don't take any for them. The rent on the first of the month, plus five quid each and I get a few basics.'

'Will you come then?' asked Nessa.

'Please. I'd like to very much, can I come on Sunday night?'

They gave her a key, took her rent money, poured another cup of tea and said that it was great to have fixed it all up so quickly. Nessa said that Jo was such a short name it would be dead easy to paint it onto the shelf in the kitchen, the shelf in the bathroom and her mug.

'She wanted to paint the names on the doors too, but I wouldn't let her,' said Pauline.

'Pauline thought it looked too much like a nursery,' said Nessa regretfully.

'Yes, and also I wanted to leave a bit of variety in life. If our names are on the doors then we'll never get any surprise visitors during the night — I always like a bit of the unexpected!'

Jo laughed too. She hoped they were joking.

*   *   *

She assured her mother in the letter that the flat was very near Haddington Road, she told her father how far it was from the damp basement, and she put in the bits about the television in each bedroom to make her sisters jealous. They had said she was an eejit to go to Dublin; the best Dublin people all came to County Clare on their holidays. She should stay at home and meet them there rather than going up and trying to find them in their own place.

*　　　*　　　*

They were having tea in the hostel on Sunday when Jo said goodbye. She struggled with her two cases to the bus stop.

'Your friends aren't going to arrange to collect you?' Sister said.

'They haven't a car, sister.'

'I see. Often, though, young people come to help a friend. I hope they are kind people, your friends.'

'Very, sister.'

'That's good. Well, God bless you, child, and remember that this is a very wicked city, a lot of very wicked people in it.'

'Yes, sister, I'll keep my eye out for them.'

It took her a long time to get to the flat.

She had to change buses twice, and was nearly exhausted when she got there. She had to come down again for the second case, and dragged the two into the room that had been pointed out as hers. It was smaller than it had looked on Friday, yet it could hardly have shrunk. The bedclothes were folded there, two blankets, two pillows and a quilt. Lord, she forgot about sheets; she'd assumed they were included. And God, she supposed there'd be no towel either, wasn't she an eejit not to have asked.

She hoped they wouldn't notice, and she'd be able

to buy some tomorrow — or she hoped she would, as she only had an hour for lunch. She'd ask one of the girls in the post office, and she had her savings for just this kind of emergency.

She hung up her clothes in the poky little wardrobe, and put out her ornaments on the window sill and her shoes in a neat line on the floor. She put her cases under the bed and sat down feeling very flat.

Back home they'd be going to the pictures or to a dance at eight o'clock on a Sunday night. In the hostel some of the girls would watch television in the lounge, others would have gone to the pictures together and go for chips on the way home, throwing the papers into the litter bin on the corner of the street where the hostel was since Sister didn't like the smell of chips coming into the building.

Nobody was sitting alone on a bed with nothing to do. She could go out and take the bus into town and go to the pictures alone, but didn't that seem ridiculous when she had her own television. Her very own. She could change the channel whenever she wanted to; she wouldn't have to ask anyone.

She was about to go out to the sitting room to see was there a Sunday paper, when she remembered there was no sitting room. She didn't want to open the doors of their rooms in case they might come in and think she was prying. She wondered where they were. Was Nessa out with a boyfriend? She hadn't mentioned one, but then girls in Dublin didn't tell you immediately if they had a fellow or not. Perhaps Pauline was at a punk disco. She couldn't believe that anyone would actually employ Pauline with that hair and let her meet the public, but maybe she was kept hidden away. Perhaps they'd come home about eleven o'clock (well, they had to get up for work in the morning); perhaps they all had cocoa or drinking chocolate in the sitting room — well, in the kitchen, to end the day. She'd tell them how well she'd settled in. In the meantime she would sit back and watch her own television set.

Jo fell asleep after half an hour. She had been very tired. She dreamed that Nessa and Pauline had come in. Pauline had decided to wash the pink out of her hair and share a room with Nessa. They were going to turn Pauline's room into a sitting room where they would sit and talk and plan. She woke suddenly when she heard giggling. It was Pauline and a man's voice, and they had gone into the kitchen.

Jo shook herself. She must have been asleep for three hours; she had a crick in her neck and the television was flickering. She stood up and turned it off, combed her hair and was about to go out and welcome the homecomers when she hesitated. If Pauline had invited a boy home presumably she was going to take him to bed with her. Perhaps the last thing she might need now was her new flatmate coming out looking for company. They were laughing in the kitchen, she could hear them, then she heard the electric kettle hiss and whistle. Well, she could always pretend that she had been going to make herself a cup of tea.

Nervously, she opened the door and went into the kitchen. Pauline was with a young man who wore a heavy leather jacket with a lot of studs on it.

'Hallo, Pauline, I was just going to get myself a cup of tea,' Jo said apologetically.

'Sure,' Pauline said. She was not unfriendly, she didn't look annoyed, but she made no effort to introduce her friend.

The kettle was still hot so Jo found a mug with

97

Visitor on it and put in a tea bag. 'Nessa's going to paint my name on a mug,' she said to the man in the jacket, just for something to say. 'Oh good,' he said. He shrugged and asked Pauline, 'Who's Nessa?'

'Lives over there,' Pauline said, indicating the direction of Nessa's room.

'I'm the third girl,' Jo said desperately. 'Third in what?' he said, genuinely bewildered. Pauline had fixed the tray of tea and biscuits and was moving towards the door.

''Night,' she said, companionably enough.

'Good night, Pauline, goodnight ... er ... ' Jo said.

She took the cup of tea into her own room. She turned up the television slightly in case she heard the sound of anything next door. She hoped she hadn't annoyed Pauline. She couldn't see what she had done that might annoy her, and anyway she had seemed cheerful enough when she was taking this boy off to — well, to her room. Jo sighed and got into bed.

*   *   *

Next morning she was coming out of the bathroom when she met Nessa.

'It's just "J" and "O", two letters, isn't it?' Nessa asked.

'Oh yes, that's right, thank you very much, Nessa.'

'Right. I didn't want to do it and then find you had an "E" on it.'

'No, no, it's short for Josephine.'

'Right on.' Nessa was off.

'What time are you coming home tonight?' Jo

asked.

'Oh, I don't think I'll have them done tonight,' Nessa said.

'I didn't mean that, I just wondered what you were doing for your tea . . . supper. You know?'

'No idea,' said Nessa cheerfully

'Oh,' said Jo. 'Sorry.'

*　　　　*　　　　*

Jacinta, who worked beside her, asked her how the flat was.

'It's great altogether,' Jo said.

'Dead right to get out of that hostel, you'd have no life in a hostel,' Jacinta said wisely.

'No, no indeed.'

'God, I wish I didn't live at home,' Jacinta said. 'It's not natural for people to live in their own homes, there should be a law about it. They have laws over stupid things like not importing live fowl, as if anyone would want to, but they have no laws about the things that people really need.'

'Yes,' said Jo dutifully.

'Anyway, you'll have the high life from now on. You country ones have all the luck.'

'I suppose we do,' Jo agreed doubtfully.

*　　　　*　　　　*

If she had stayed in the hostel they might have been playing twenty-five in the lounge now, or someone might have bought a new record. They would look at the evening paper, sigh over the price of flats, wonder whether to go the pictures and complain about the food. There would be talk and endless tea or bottles of coke from the machine. There would not be four walls as there were now.

She had bought a hamburger on the way home and eaten it. She washed her tights, she put the new sheets on the bed and hung her new towel up in the bathroom on the third hook. The other hooks had 'N' and 'P' on them. She took out her writing pad but remembered that she had written home on Friday just after she had found the flat. There was nothing new to tell. The evening yawned ahead of her. And then there would be Tuesday and Wednesday and Thursday ... Tears came into her eyes and fell down on to her lap as she sat on the end of her bed. She must be absolutely awful to have no friends and nowhere to go and nothing to do. Other people of eighteen had great times. She used to have great times when she was seventeen, at school and planning to be eighteen. Look at her now, sitting alone. Even her flat mates didn't want to have anything to do with her. She cried and cried. Then she got a headache so she took two aspirins and climbed into bed. It's bloody fantastic being grown up, she thought, as she switched off the light at nine o'clock.

*   *   *

There was 'J' on her towel rack, her name was on the bathroom shelf that belonged to her, and her empty kitchen shelf had a 'Jo' on it also. She examined the other two shelves. Nessa had cornflakes and a packet of sugar and a lot of tins of soup on her shelf. Pauline had a biscuit tin and about a dozen tins of grapefruit segments on hers.

The kitchen was nice and tidy. Nessa had said the first day that they never left any washing up to be done and that if you used the frying pan you had to scrub it then, not let it steep until the morning. It had all seemed great fun when she was talking about it then, because Jo had envisaged midnight feasts, and all three of them laughing and having parties. That's what people *did*, for heaven's sake. She must have just got in with two recluses, that was her problem.

Pauline came in to the kitchen yawning, and opened a tin of grapefruit segments. 'I think I'd never wake up if I didn't have these,' she said. 'I have half a tin and two biscuits for my breakfast every day, and then I'm ready for anything.'

Jo was pleased to be spoken to.

'Is your friend here?' she said, trying to be modern and racey.

'Which friend?' Pauline yawned and began to spoon the grapefruit out of the tin into a bowl.

'You know, your friend, the other night?'

'Nessa?' Pauline looked at her blankly. 'Do you mean Nessa?'

'No, the fellow, the fellow with the jacket with the studs. I met him here in the kitchen.'

'Oh yes. Shane.'

'Shane. That was his name.'

'Yeah, what about him, what were you saying?'

'I was asking was he here?'

'Here? Now? Why should he be here?' Pauline pushed her pink hair out of her eyes and looked at her watch. 'Jesus Christ, it's only twenty to eight in the morning, why would he be here?' She looked wildly around the kitchen as if the man with the studded leather jacket was going to appear from behind the gas cooker. Jo felt the conversation was going wrong.

'I just asked sociably if he was still here, that was

all.'

'But why on earth would he be still here? I went out with him on Sunday night. *Sunday*. It's Tuesday morning now, isn't it? Why would he be here?' Pauline looked confused and worried, and Jo wished she had never spoken.

'I just thought he was your boyfriend . . . '

'No, he's not, but if he was I tell you I wouldn't have him here at twenty to eight in the morning talking! I don't know how anyone can talk in the mornings. It beats me.'

Jo drank her tea silently.

'See you,' said Pauline eventually when she had finished her biscuits and grapefruit, and crashed into the bathroom.

Jo thanked Nessa for putting up the names. Nessa was pleased. 'I like doing that, it gives me a sense of order in the world. It defines things, that makes me feel better.'

'Sure,' said Jo. She was just about to ask Nessa what she was doing that evening when she remembered yesterday's rebuff. She decided to phrase it differently this time.

'Are you off out with your friends this evening?' she said timidly.

'I might be, I might not, it's always hard to know in the morning, isn't it?'

'Yes it is,' said Jo untruthfully. It was becoming increasingly easy to know in the morning, she thought. The answer was coming up loud and clear when she asked herself what she was going to do in the evening. The answer was Nothing.

'Well I'm off now. Goodbye,' she said to Nessa.

Nessa looked up and smiled. 'Bye bye,' she said vaguely, as if Jo had been the postman or the man delivering milk on the street.

*　　　*　　　*

On Thursday night Jo went downstairs to answer the phone. It was for one of the nurses on the ground floor as it always was. Hesitantly she knocked on their door. The big blonde nurse thanked her, and as Jo was going up the stairs again she heard the girl say, 'No, it was one of the people in the flats upstairs. There's three flats upstairs and we all share the same phone.'

That was it! That was what she hadn't realised. She wasn't in a flat with two other girls, she was in a flat by herself. Why hadn't that dawned on her? She was in a proper bedsitter all of her own, she just shared kitchen and bathroom facilities, as they would put it in an ad. That's what had been wrong. She had thought that she was meant to be part of a jolly all-girls-together. That's why she had been so depressed. She went over the whole conversation with Nessa the first day; she remembered what they had said about doing it up as bedsitters but not telling the landlord anything, it never did to tell landlords anything, just keep paying the rent and keep out of his way.

There was quite a bounce in her step now. I'm on my own in Dublin, she thought, I have my own place, I'm going out to find a life for myself now. She didn't have to worry about Pauline's morals any more now. If Pauline wanted to bring home a rough-looking person with studs on his jacket that was Pauline's business. She just lived in the flat next door. That's what Pauline had meant when she had said Nessa lived next door. And that's why Nessa went in for all this labelling and naming things. No wonder they had been slightly surprised when she kept asking them what they were doing in the evening; they must have thought she was mad.

Happy for the first time since Sunday, Jo did herself up. She put on eyeshadow and mascara, she put some colour in her cheeks and wore her big earrings. She didn't know where she was going, but she decided that she would go out cheerfully now. She looked around her room and liked it much better. She would get some posters for the walls, she would even ask her mother if she could take some of the ornaments from home. The kitchen shelves at home were chock-a-block with ornaments; her mother would be glad to give some of them a new home. Humming happily, she set off.

She felt terrific as she swung along with her shoulderbag. She pitied her sisters who were only finishing the late shift now at the hotel. She pitied the girls who still had to stay in a hostel, who hadn't been able to go out and find a place of their own. She felt sorry for Jacinta who had to stay at home and whose mother and father interrogated her about where she went and what she did. She pitied people who had to share television sets. What if you wanted to look at one thing and they wanted to look at something else? How did you decide? She was so full of good spirits that she nearly walked past the pub where the notice said: 'Tonight — the Great Gaels.'

Imagine, the Great Gaels were there in person. In a pub. Cover charge £1. If she paid a pound she would see them close up. Up to now she had only seen them on television.

They had been at the Fleadh in Ennis once about four years ago, before they were famous. She had seen an advertisement, all right, saying that they would be in this pub, and now here she was outside it. Jo's heart beat fast. Was it a thing you could do on your own, go into a concert in a pub? Probably it was a thing people went to in groups; she might look odd. Maybe there'd be no place for just one person to sit. Maybe it would only be tables for groups.

But a great surge of courage came flooding over her. She was a young woman who lived in a flat on her own in Dublin, she had her own place and by the Lord, if she could do that, she could certainly go into a pub and hear the Great Gaels on her own. She pushed the door.

A man sat at the desk inside and gave her a cloak-room ticket and took her pound.

'Where do I go?' she almost whispered.

'For what?' he asked.

'You know, where exactly do I go?' she asked. It seemed like an ordinary pub to her, no stage, maybe the Great Gaels were upstairs.

The man assumed she was looking for the Ladies. 'I think it's over there near the other door, yes, there it is beside the Gents.' He pointed across the room.

Flushing a dark red she thanked him. In case he was still looking at her she thought she had better go to the Ladies. In the cloakroom she looked at her face. It had looked fine at home, back in her flat. In here it looked a bit dull, no character, no colour. She put on much more makeup in the dim light and came out to find out where the concert would be held.

She saw two women sitting together. They looked safe enough to ask. They told her with an air of surprise that it would be in the pub, but not for about an hour.

'What do we do until then?' she asked.

They laughed. 'I suppose you could consider

having a drink, it is a pub after all,' said one of them. They went back to their conversation. She felt very silly. She didn't want to leave and come back in case there was no re-admittance. She wished she had brought a paper or a book. Everyone else seemed to be talking.

She sat for what seemed like a very long time. Twice the waiter asked her would she be having another drink as he cleaned around her glass of orange, which she was ekeing out. She didn't want to waste too much money; a pound already coming in was enough to spend.

Then people arrived and started to fix up microphones, and the crowd was bigger suddenly and she was squeezed towards the end of the seat, and she saw the Great Gaels having pints up at the bar just as if they were ordinary customers. Wasn't Dublin fantastic? You could go into a pub and sit and have a drink in the same place as the Great Gaels. They'd never believe her at home.

The lead singer of the Great Gaels was tapping the microphone and testing it by saying, *'a haon, a dhó, a trí . . .'* Everyone laughed and settled down with full drinks.

'Come on now, attention please, we don't want anyone with an empty glass now getting up and disturbing us,' he said.

'Divil a fear of that,' someone shouted.

'All right, look around you. If you see anyone who might be fidgety, fill up their glass for them.'

Two men beside Jo looked at her glass disapprovingly. 'What have you in there, Miss?' one said.

'Orange, but it's fine, I won't get up and disturb them,' she said, hating to be the centre of attention.

'Large gin and orange for the lady,' one man said.

'Oh no,' called Jo, 'It's not gin . . .'

'Sorry. Large vodka and orange for the lady,' he corrected.

'Right,' said the waiter, eyeing her disapprovingly, Jo felt.

When it came she had her purse out.

'Nonsense, I bought you a drink,' said the man.

'Oh, but you can't do that,' she said.

He paid what seemed like a fortune for it; Jo looked into the glass nervously.

'It was very expensive, wasn't it?' she said.

'Well, that's the luck of the draw, you might have been a beer drinker,' he smiled at her. He was very old, over thirty, and his friend was about the same.

Jo wished they hadn't bought the drink. She wasn't used to accepting drinks. Should she offer to buy the next round? Would they accept, or would they worse still buy her another? Perhaps she should just accept this one and move a bit away from them. But wasn't that awfully rude? Anyway, now with the Great Gaels about to begin, she wouldn't have to talk to them.

'Thank you very much indeed,' she said putting the orange into the large vodka. 'That's very nice of you, and most generous.'

'Not at all,' said the man with the open-neck shirt.

'It'sh a pleashure,' said the other man.

Then she realised that they were both very drunk.

The Great Gaels had started, but Jo couldn't enjoy them. She felt this should have been a great night, only twenty feet away from Ireland's most popular singers, in a nice, warm pub, and a free drink in her hand, what more could a girl want? But to her great embarrassment the man with the open-neck shirt had settled himself so that his arm was along the back of the seat behind her, and from time to time it would drop round her shoulder. His friend was beating his feet to the music with such energy that a lot of his pint had already spilled on the floor.

Jo hoped fervently that they wouldn't make a scene, and that if they did nobody would think that they were with her. She had a horror of drunks ever since the time that her Uncle Jim had taken up the leg of lamb and thrown it into the fire because somebody crossed him when they had all been invited to a meal. The evening had broken up in a shambles and as they went home her father had spoken about drink being a good servant but a cruel master. Her father had said that Uncle Jim was two people, one drunk and one sober, and they were as unlike as you could find. Her father said that it was a mercy that Uncle Jim's weakness hadn't been noticeable in any of the rest of the family, and her mother had been very upset and said they had all thought Jim was cured.

Sometimes her sisters told her terrible things people had done in the hotel when they were drunk. Drunkenness was something frightening and unknown. And now she had managed to land herself in a corner with a drunk's arm around her.

The Great Gaels played encore after encore, and they only stopped at closing time. Jo had now received another large vodka and orange from the friend of the open-shirted man, and when she had tried to refuse, he had said, 'You took one from Gerry — what's wrong with my drink?'

She had been so alarmed by his attitude she had rushed to drink it.

The Great Gaels were selling copies of their latest record, and autographing it as well. She would have loved to have bought it in some ways, to remind herself that she had been right beside them, but then it would have reminded her of Gerry and Christy, and the huge vodkas which were making her legs feel funny, and the awful fact that the evening was not over yet.

'I tried to buy you a drink to say thank you for all you bought me, but the bar man told me it's after closing time,' she said nervously.

'It is now?' said Gerry. 'Isn't that a bit of bad news.'

'Imagine, the girl didn't get a chance to buy us a drink,' said Christy.

'That's unfortunate,' said Gerry.

'Most unfortunate,' said Christy.

'Maybe I could meet you another night and buy you one?' She looked anxiously from one to another. 'Would that be all right?'

'That would be quite all right, it would be excellent,' said Gerry.

'But what would be more excellent,' said Christy, 'would be if you invited us home for a cup of coffee.'

'Maybe the girl lives with her Mam and Dad,' said Gerry.

'No, I live on my own,' said Jo proudly and then could have bitten off her tongue.

'Well now,' Gerry brightened. 'That would be a nice way to round off the evening.'

'I don't have any more drink though, I wouldn't have any beer . . . '

'That's all right, we have a little something to put in the coffee.' Gerry was struggling into his coat.

'Are you far from here?' Christy was asking.

'Only about ten minutes' walk.' Her voice was hardly above a whisper. Now that she had let them know that the coast was clear, she could think of not one way of stopping them. 'It's a longish ten minutes, though,' she said.

'That'll clear our heads, a nice walk,' said Christy.

'Just what we need,' said Gerry.

Would they rape her? she wondered. Would they assume that this was why she was inviting them back — so that she could have sexual intercourse with both of them? Probably. And then if she resisted they would say she was only leading them on and insist on having their way with her. Was she stark staring mad? She cleared her throat.

'It's only coffee, mind, that's all,' she said in a schoolmistressy way.

'Sure, that's fine, that's what you said,' Christy said. 'I have a naggin of whiskey in my pocket. I told you.'

They walked down the road. Jo was miserable. How had she got herself into this? She knew that she *could* turn to them in the brightly lit street and say, 'I'm sorry, I've changed my mind, I have to be up early tomorrow morning.' She *could* say, 'Oh heavens, I forgot, my mother is coming tonight, I totally forgot, she wouldn't like me bringing people in when she's asleep.' She *could* say that the landlord didn't let them have visitors. But she felt that it needed greater courage to say any of them than to plod on to whatever was going to happen.

Gerry and Christy were happy, they did little dance steps to some of the songs they sang, and made her join in a chorus of the last song the Great Gaels had sung. People looked at them on the street and smiled. Jo had never felt so wretched in her whole life.

At the door she asked them to hush. And they did in an exaggerated way, putting their fingers on their lips and saying 'shush' to each other. She let them in and they went upstairs. Please, please God, may Nessa and Pauline not be in the kitchen. They never are any other night, let them not be there tonight.

They were both there. Nessa in a dressing gown, Pauline in a great black waterproof cape; she was colouring her hair apparently, and didn't want bits of the gold to fall on her clothes.

Jo smiled a stiff 'good evening' and tried to manipulate the two men past the door.

'More lovely girls, more lovely girls,' said Gerry delightedly. 'You said you lived by yourself.'

'I do,' snapped Jo. 'These are the girls from next door, we share a kitchen.'

'I see,' Pauline said in a huffed tone. 'Downgraded.'

Jo wasn't going to explain. If only she could get the two drunks into her own bed-sitter.

'What are you doing, is that a fancy-dress?' Christy asked Pauline.

'No, it's not a fancy-dress, wise guy, it's my night-dress — I always go to bed in a black sou'wester,' Pauline said and everyone except Jo screeched with laughter.

'I was just going to make us some coffee,' said Jo sharply, taking down three mugs with Visitor painted on them. Gerry thought the mugs were the funniest thing he had ever seen.

'Why do you put Visitor on them?' he asked Jo.

'I have no idea,' Jo said. 'Ask Nessa.'

'So that you'll remember you're visitors and won't move in,' Nessa said. They all found this very funny too.

'If you'd like to go into my bedroom — my flat, I mean, I'll follow with the coffees,' Jo said.

'It's great crack here,' said Christy and produced his small bottle from his hip pocket.

Nessa and Pauline got their mugs immediately.

In no time they were all friends. Christy took out a bit of paper and wrote Christy and Gerry and they stuck the names to their mugs — so that they would feel part of the gang, he said. Jo felt the vodka and the heat and the stress had been too much for her. Unsteadily she got to her feet and staggered to the bathroom. She felt so weak afterwards that she couldn't face the kitchen again. She went to the misery of her bed, and oblivion.

She felt terrible in the morning. She couldn't understand why people like Uncle Jim had wanted to drink. Drinking made other people ridiculous and made you feel sick, how could anyone like it? She remembered slowly, like a slow-motion film, the events of the night before and her cheeks reddened with shame. They would probably ask her to leave. Imagine coming home with two drunks, and then abandoning them in the kitchen while she had gone away to be sick. God knows who they were, those two men, Gerry and Christy. They might have been burglars even . . . Jo sat up in bed. Or suppose when she had disappeared . . . suppose they had attacked Nessa and Pauline?

She leapt out of bed, uncaring about her headache and her stomach cramps, and burst out of her door. The kitchen was its usual tidy self: all the mugs washed and hanging back on their hooks. Trembling, she opened the doors of their bedrooms. Pauline's room was the same as ever — huge posters on the wall and a big long clothes rail, like you'd see in a shop that sold dresses, where Pauline hung all her gear. Nessa's room was neat as a pin, candlewick bedspread, chest of drawers, with photographs neatly arranged; little hanging bookshelf with about twenty paperbacks on it. No sign of rape or struggle in either room.

Jo looked at her watch; she was going to be late for work, the others had obviously gone ages ago. But why had they left her no note? No explanation? Or a note asking her for an explanation?

Jo staggered to work, to the wrath that met her as she was forty minutes late. Jacinta said to her at one stage that she looked pretty ropey.

'Pretty ropey is exactly how I feel. I think I'm having my first hangover.'

'Well for you,' said Jacinta jealously. 'I never get a chance to do anything that might give me even a small hangover.'

She was dreading going home. Over and over she rehearsed her apologies. She would put it down to the drink. Or would that be worse? Would they find her even more awful if they thought she was so drunk last night she didn't know what she was doing? Would she say she had been introduced to them by a friend, so she thought they were respectable and when she found out they weren't it was too late? What would she say? Just that she was sorry.

Neither of them were there. She waited for ages but they didn't come in. She wrote out a note and left it on the kitchen table. 'I'm very very sorry about last night. Please wake me when you come in and I will try to give you an explanation. Jo.'

But nobody woke her, and when she did wake it was Saturday morning. Her note was still on the table. They hadn't bothered to wake her. She was so despicable they didn't even want to discuss it.

She made her morning cup of tea and stole back to bed. It was lunchtime before she realised that neither of them was in the flat. They mustn't have come home.

Jo had never felt so uneasy in her life. There must be a perfectly reasonable explanation. After all, there had been no arrangement to tell any of the others their movements. She had realised this on Thursday night. They all lived separate lives. But what could have happened that they had disappeared? Jo told herself that she was being ridiculous. Nessa lived in Waterford, or her family did, so she had probably gone home for the weekend. Pauline was from the country too, somewhere. Well, she had to be, otherwise she wouldn't be in a flat. She'd probably gone home too.

It was just a coincidence that they had gone the same weekend. And just a coincidence that they had gone after the visit of the two drunks.

Jo stood up and sat down again. Of course they had to be at home with their families. What else was she imagining? Go on, spell it out, what do you fear, she said to herself, that those two innocent-looking eejits who had a bit too much to drink kidnapped two big strong girls like Pauline and Nessa? Come on! Yes, it was ridiculous, it was ludicrous. What did they do, hold them at gun point while they tidied up the flat and then pack them into a van and bear them off?

Jo had often been told she had a vivid imagination. This was an occasion when she could have done without it. But it wouldn't go away. She couldn't pull a curtain over the worries, the pictures that kept coming up of Christy hitting Nessa and of Gerry strangling Pauline, and all through her mind went the refrain, 'There must be something wrong, otherwise they would have left me a note.'

It was her fourth Saturday in Dublin. The first one she had spent unpacking her case and getting used to the hostel; the second one had been spent looking at flats which were too expensive and too far from work, and which had already been taken by other people; the third Saturday she had spent congratulating herself on having found Nessa and Pauline; and now on this, the fourth Saturday, Nessa and Pauline had most likely been brutally murdered and ravaged by two drunks that she had brought back to the flat. How could she explain it to anyone? 'Well, you see, it was like this, Sergeant. I had two double vodkas in the pub bought by these men, and then when we came home – oh yes, sergeant, I brought them home with me, why not? Well, when we came home they poured whiskey into our coffees and before I knew where I was I had passed out in a stupor and when I woke up my flat-mates were gone, and they never came back. They were never seen again.'

Jo cried and cried. They *must* have gone home for the weekend. People did. She had read a big article in the paper not long ago about these fellows making a fortune driving people home in a minibus; apparently lots of country girls missed the crack at home at weekends. They must have gone off in a minibus. Please, please St Jude, may they have gone in a minibus. If they went in a minibus, St Jude, I'll never do anything bad for the rest of my life. More than that. More. If they're definitely safe and they went off yesterday in a minibus, St Jude, I'll tell everyone about you. I'll put a notice in the two evening papers – and the three daily papers, too, if it wasn't too dear. She would bring St Jude's name into casual conversation with people and say that he was a great man in a crisis. She wouldn't actually describe the whole crisis in detail, of course. Oh dear Lord, speak,

speak, should she go to the guards? Should she report it or was she making the most ludicrous fuss over nothing? Would Pauline and Nessa be furious if the guards contacted their homes? God, suppose they'd gone off with fellows or something? Imagine, if the guards were calling on their families? She'd have the whole country alerted for nothing.

But if she didn't get the guards, suppose something had happened because of those drunk men she'd invited into the house, yes, she, Josephine Margaret Assumpta O'Brien had invited two drunk men into a house, not a week after that nun in the hostel had said that Dublin was a very wicked city, and now her two flatmates, innocent girls who had done nothing to entice these men in, were missing, with no trace of them whatsoever . . .

She had nothing to eat for the day. She walked around hugging herself, stopping when she heard the slightest sound in case it might be a key in the lock. When it was getting dark she remembered how they had written their names on bits of paper: they could have taken them away with them, but they might be in the rubbish bin. Yes, there they were, Christy and Gerry, scrawled on paper with bits of sellotape attached to it. Jo took them out with a fork in case they might still have fingerprints on them. She put them on the kitchen table and said a decade of the rosary beside them.

Outside people passed in the street going about the business of a Saturday night. Was it only last Saturday that she had gone to the pictures with Josie and Helen, those two nice girls in the hostel? Why hadn't she stayed there? It had been awful since she left, it had been frightening and worrying and getting worse every day until . . . until This.

There was nobody she could talk to. Suppose she phoned her sister in the hotel, Dymphna would be furious with her; the immediate reaction would be, come-home-at-once, what-are-you-doing-by-yourself-up-in-Dublin, everyone-knew-you-couldn't-cope. And it was a temptation to run away. What time was the evening train to Limerick? Or tomorrow morning? But she didn't want to go home, and she didn't want to talk to Dymphna and she couldn't explain the whole thing on the phone downstairs in the hall in case the people in the flat below heard — the people in the flat below! *That* was it!

She was half-way down the stairs when she paused. Suppose everything were all right, and suppose St Jude had got them on a minibus, wouldn't Nessa and Pauline be furious if she had gone in and alarmed the three nurses downstairs? They had said that they kept themselves very much to themselves; the nurses were all right but it didn't do to get too involved with them. Yes, well, going in and telling them that you suspected Nessa and Pauline had been abducted and maltreated was certainly getting involved.

She went back up the stairs. Was there anything that the nurses could do to help that she couldn't do? Answer: No.

Just at that moment the big blonde nurse that she had spoken to came out. 'Hey, I was just going to go up to you lot above.'

'Oh, really, what's wrong?' Jo said.

'Nothing's wrong, nothing at all, we're having a party tonight, though, and we just wanted to say if any of you lot wanted to come, it starts at . . . well, when the pubs close.'

'That's very nice of you. I don't think . . . '

'Well, all we wanted to say is, there may be a bit of

noise, but you're very welcome. If you could bring a bottle it would be a help.'

'A bottle?' asked Jo.

'Well, you don't have to, but a drop of wine would be a help.' The nurse was about to walk past her up the stairs.

'Where are you going?' Jo asked, alarmed.

'I've just told you, to ask the others, the ones in the other flats, if they'd like to come . . . '

'They're not there, they're not at home, they're gone away.'

'Oh well, all for the best, I suppose,' the girl shrugged. 'I've got my meat and my manners now, can't say they weren't asked.'

'Listen,' Jo said urgently, 'what's your name?'

'Phyllis,' she said.

'Phyllis, listen to me, do the girls up here go away a lot?'

'What?'

'I mean, I'm new here, do they go home for the weekends or anything?'

'Search me. I hardly know them at all. I think the punk one's a bit odd a half-wit, between ourselves.'

'But do they go away at weekends or what? Please, it's important.'

'Honestly, I'd never notice, I'm on nights a lot of the time, I don't know where I am or whether people are coming or going. Sorry.'

'Would the others know, in your flat?'

'I don't think so, why? Is anything wrong?'

'No, I expect not. It's just, well, I wasn't expecting them to go off and they, sort of, have. I was just wondering whether . . . you know, if everything's all right.'

'Why wouldn't it be?'

'It's just that they were with some rather, well, unreliable people on Thursday, and . . . '

'They're lucky they were only with unreliable people on Thursday, I'm with unreliable people all the time! Maureen was meant to have hired the glasses and she didn't, so we had to buy paper cups which cost a fortune.'

Jo started to go back upstairs.

'See you later then. What's your name?'

'Jo O'Brien.'

'OK, come on down when you hear the sounds.'

'Thank you.'

*   *   *

At twelve o'clock she was wider awake than she had ever been in the middle of the day; she thought she might as well go down as stay where she was. The noise was almost in the room with her. There was no question of sleep. She put on her black dress and her big earrings, then she took them off. Suppose her flat-mates were in danger or dead? What was she doing dressing up and going to a party? It somehow wasn't so bad going to a party without dressing up. She put on her grey skirt and her dark grey sweater, and went down stairs.

She arrived at the same time as four others who had been beating on the hall door. Jo opened it and let them in.

'Which are you?' said one of the men.

'I'm from upstairs, really,' Jo said.

'Right,' said the man, 'let's you and I go back upstairs, see you later,' he laughed to the others.

'No, no, you can't do that, stop it,' Jo shouted.

'It was a joke, silly,' he said.

'She thought you meant it!' The others fell about laughing. Then the door of the downstairs flat opened and a blast of heat and noise came out. There were about forty people crammed into the rooms. Jo took one look and was about to scamper upstairs again, but it was too late and the door had banged behind her. Someone handed her a glass of warm wine. She saw Phyllis in the middle of it all, her blonde hair tied in a top knot and wearing a very dazzling dress with bootlace straps. Jo felt foolish and shabby: she was jammed into a group of bright-faced, laughing people and she felt as grey as her jumper and skirt.

'Are you a nurse too?' a boy asked her.

'No, I work in the post office.'

'Well, can you do anything about the telephones, do you know there isn't a telephone between here and . . . '

'I don't give a damn about telephones,' she said and pushed away from him. Nessa and Pauline were dead, battered by drunks, and here she was talking about telephones to some fool.

'I was only making conversation — piss off,' he shouted at her, hurt.

Nobody heard him in the din.

'Which are your flatmates?' Jo asked Phyllis.

'The one in the kitchen, Maureen, and the one dancing with the man in the aran sweater, that's Mary.'

'Thanks,' said Jo. She went into the kitchen.

'Maureen,' she said. The girl at the cooker looked up with an agonised face. 'I wanted to ask you . . . '

'Burned to a crisp, both of them. Both of them burned to a bloody crisp.'

'What?' said Jo.

'Two trays of sausages. Just put them in the oven,

stop fussing, Mary says. I put them in the oven. And now look, burned black. Jesus, do you know how much sausages are a pound, and there were five pounds altogether. I told her we should have fried them. Stink the place out, frying them, she said. Well, what will this do, I ask you?'

'Do you know the girls upstairs?' Jo persisted.

'No, but Phyllis said she asked them, they're not making trouble are they? That's all we need.'

'No, I'm one of them, that's not the problem.'

'Thank God. What will I do with this?'

'Throw it out dish and all, I'd say, you'll never clean it.'

'Yes, you're right. God, what a fiasco. What a mess.'

'Listen, do you know the girls, the other ones, Nessa and Pauline?'

'Just to see. Why?'

'Do you know where they are?'

'What? Of course I don't. If they're here they're in the other room, I suppose, waiting to be fed, thinking there's some hot food. I'll *kill* Mary, I'll literally *kill* her, you know.'

'Do they normally go away for the weekend?'

'God, love, I don't know whether they go up to the moon and back for the weekend. How would I know? There's one of them with a head like a lighthouse and another who goes round with that dynatape thing putting names on anything that stands still . . . bells and doors and things. I think they're all right. We never have many dealings with them. That's the best way in a house of flats, I always say.'

Jo left it there. It seemed unlikely that Mary would know any more, and she decided to leave her happily with the man in the aran sweater until she was given the bad news about the sausages.

A hand caught her and suddenly she was dancing herself. The man was tall and had a nice smile.

'Where are you from, Limerick?'

'Not far out,' she said laughing. Then dread seized her again. What was she doing dancing with this stranger and chatting him up like she might have done at a dance at home? 'I'm sorry,' she said to him, 'I'm sorry, I have to go. I've got something awful on my mind, I can't stay.'

At that moment the window in the kitchen was broken by a big stone, and glass shattered everywhere. There were screams from the garden and shouts.

'I'm getting the guards, this looks like a bad fight,' said the tall boy and like a flash he was out in the hall. Jo heard him speaking on the phone. In the kitchen people were shouting to each other to move carefully. A huge lump of glass lay precariously on top of a cupboard: it could fall any moment.

'Is anybody hurt, stop screaming, is anybody cut?' Jo recognised Phyllis and felt a small amount of relief flood back into her. At least they were nurses; maybe a lot of them were. They'd be able to cope better than ordinary people. People had run out the front door and an almighty row was going on in the garden. Two men with cut heads were shouting that they only threw the stone in self-defence, people had started firing things at them from the window first; one of them was bleeding over his eye. They only picked up the stone to stop the barrage coming at them.

The guards were there very quickly, four of them. Suddenly everything was different; what had looked like a party began to look like something shameful. The room that had been full of smoke and drink and music and people dancing and people talking about nothing was now a room full of broken glass and upturned chairs and people shouting trying to explain what had happened, and people trying to comfort others, or get their coats and leave. Neighbours had come to protest and to stare: it was all different.

It didn't take long to work it out: the two men in the garden were crashers. They had tried to come in the front door and been refused admittance; they had then gone around to see if there was a back entrance. That was when the first one had been attacked with a hot weapon which had both burned and cut his face. Investigating the attack, the other one had been wounded in exactly the same way. (The weapons were, of course, Mary's burnt sausages.) They thought that everybody in the party was firing things at them so they threw one stone before leaving.

Notebooks were being put away. Phyllis said that one of the men needed a stitch, and she would go to the hospital with him, taking Mary as well, since Mary's arm had been cut by flying glass. The party was over. The guards said that too much noise was being made for a built-up area and, since two of the hostesses were disappearing to the hospital, there didn't seem to be any point in guests staying on in a flat which was now full of icy winds because of the window. Some of the men helped to pick the last bit of broken glass out, and a sheet of tin was found in the boot of somebody's car. It was a sorry end. The guards were leaving; one of them saw Jo sitting on the stairs.

'Are you all right for a lift home?' he asked.

Jo shook her head. 'I don't need one. I live upstairs.'

'You look a bit shook, are you all right?'

She nodded wordlessly.

'What a night, not much of a Saturday night in Dublin for a little country girl, is it?'

He was trying to cheer her up. It didn't work.

'Well, I'll be off, you go off too and get some sleep, you need it by the look of you.'

She nodded again.

'You are all right, you're not in shock or anything? It's all over, it was only a broken window,' he said soothingly. 'There'll be worse than that before the night's over.'

'Oh God,' she said.

'Hey, Sean,' he called, 'this one's going to faint, I think, give me a hand.'

She came to as they were getting her in the door of the flat. She had had the key in her hand and it had fallen when she fell.

'Which is her room?' Sean said.

'How would I know?' said the one who was carrying her. 'Here's the kitchen, get her in there . . . '

She saw the names on the table.

'Don't touch those, they're evidence,' she said. 'Please don't touch them.'

They decided they'd better all have a cup of tea.

*　　　*　　　*

'It's television, that's what it is,' Mickey said.

'It's that and eating too much rich food late at night,' said Sean.

'But how can you be sure they're all right?' Jo wasn't convinced.

'Because we're normal human beings,' said Sean.

Jo flushed. 'So am I. I'm normal too, that's why I'm worried. I'm just concerned and worried about them. Stop making horrible jokes about my eating rich food and having nightmares. I haven't eaten anything, I'm so worried, and that is exactly why I didn't come to the Garda station because I knew that's the kind of reception I'd get.'

She burst into tears and put her head down on the table.

'Mind the evidence,' Sean giggled

Mickey frowned at him. 'Leave her alone, she *is* worried. Listen here, those two will be back tomorrow night right as rain. Nobody abducts people like that, honestly. Nobody says please wash up all the mugs and tidy up your rooms and come on up the Dublin mountains to be abducted, now do they?' He smiled at her encouragingly.

'I suppose they wouldn't.'

'And you are kind to be concerned, and we'll say no more about it tonight now because you're exhausted. Go to sleep and have a lie in tomorrow. Those two rossies will be home tomorrow night and you'll think you were mad crying your heart out over them. Do you hear me?'

'But I'm so stupid, I'm so hopeless. I can't cope with Dublin, I really can't. I thought I'd have a great time when I got a flat, but it's all so different, and so lonely, so terribly lonely, and when it isn't lonely it's like a nightmare . . . '

'Now stop that,' Mickey said firmly. 'Stop it at once. You never talk about anyone but yourself, I this, I that. You're constantly wondering what people are thinking about you. They're not thinking about you at all.'

'But I . . . '

'There you go again. I, I, I. You think that there's some kind of gallery of people watching you, sitting there as if they were at the pictures, watching you leave the house each day, all your movements, saying, is she having a good time, is she being a success in Dublin? Nobody gives one damn. Why don't you start thinking about other people?'

'But I *am* thinking about other people, I'm thinking about Nessa and Pauline . . . '

'Oh no, you're not, you're only thinking about what *you* did to them, whether *you're* responsible for their kidnapping and disappearance, or whether they'll think *you're* silly.'

Jo looked at him.

'So, lecture over. Go to sleep.' He stood up. So did Sean.

'You're probably right,' she said.

'He's always right, known for it,' said Sean.

'Thank you very much indeed, it is a bit lonely at first, you get self-centred.'

'I know, I felt a bit the same last year.'

'Sligo?'

'Galway.'

'Thank you very much again.'

'Goodbye, Jo.'

'Goodbye, Guard, thank you.'

'Mickey,' he said.

'Mickey,' she said.

'And Sean,' Sean said.

'And Sean,' Jo said.

'And maybe some night you might come out with me,' said Mickey.

'Or me, indeed?' said Sean.

'I saw her first, didn't I?' said Mickey.

'You did,' said Jo. 'Indeed you did.'

'I'll wait a bit until the two lassies are back and installed, but I've a night off on Monday . . . '

'You're sure they'll come back?'

'Maybe if I called for you about eight on Monday? How's that?'

'That's grand,' said Jo. 'That's grand altogether.'

DECISION IN BELFIELD

III

She had been reading the Problem Pages for years.
One or two of them always said things about having
done grievous wrong in the eyes of God and now the
only thing to do was to Make Restitution. Most of
them said that your parents would be very understanding — you must go straight away and tell them.
You will be surprised, the Problem Pages said, at
how much tolerance and understanding there will
be, and how much support there is to be found at
home.

Not in Pat's home. There would be no support
there, no understanding. Pat's mother wasn't going
to smile like people did in movies and say maybe
it was all for the best and it would be nice to have
another baby around the place, that she had missed
the patter of tiny bootees. And Pat's father wasn't
going to put his arm around her shoulder and take
her for a long supportive walk on Dun Laoghaire
pier. Pat knew all this very well, even though the
Problem Pages told her she was wrong. But she knew
it from personal experience. She knew that Mum
and Dad would not be a bundle of support and two
big rocks of strength. Because they hadn't been any
of that five years ago when her elder sister Cathy had
been pregnant. There was no reason why their
attitude should have changed as time went by.

Cathy had actually finished college when her little drama broke on the family. She had been twenty-two years old, earning her own living and in most ways living her own life. Cathy had believed the Problem Pages, she thought that Mum wouldn't go through the roof. Cathy had thought that there were ways you could talk to Mum and Dad like ordinary people. She had been wrong. Pat remembered as if it were yesterday the weekend of the announcement. It seemed to have gone on all weekend, Cathy saying she didn't want to marry Ian and Dad saying Ian must be brought around to the house this minute; Mum saying this was the result of trusting people to behave like adults and like responsible people; Cathy looking frightened and bewildered. She had said over and over that she thought people would be pleased.

Pat had been sixteen, and she had been shocked to the core. She had never heard words used like the words that were used that weekend. Dad had even apologised for some of the things he had called Cathy, and Mum had never stopped crying. Cathy came and sat on her bed on the Sunday evening. 'It's not the end of the world,' she had said.

'Oh, but it is,' Pat had said, almost afraid to look at Cathy in case she saw under her waist the whole dreadful shame that was going to cause such trouble.

'It's just that I can't see myself spending the rest of my life with Ian,' Cathy said. 'We'd be ridiculous together, we wouldn't last a year. It's such a terrible way to start a marriage with anyone.'

'But don't you love him?' Pat had asked. The only possible reason you could do the things that Cathy must have done with Ian to get herself to this stage must have been love.

'Oh yes, in a way, I love him, but I'll love

other people and so will he.'

Pat had not understood, she had been no help. She had said useless things like maybe it wasn't really positive, the test, and maybe Ian might like to get married if Cathy explained it properly. Cathy had taken the whole thing very badly; she had refused to accept that Mum and Dad might have any right on their side. 'They're so liberal, they *say* they're so liberal,' she had scoffed. 'They keep saying they're in favour of getting divorce introduced and they want contraceptives, and they want censorship abolished, but they refuse to face facts. They want me to marry a man knowing it will ruin my life and ruin his life, and probably wreck the baby's life as well. What kind of liberal view is that?'

'I think they believe that it would be the best start for the . . . er . . . the child,' said Pat uncertainly.

'Great start . . . forcing two people who should love the child most into a marriage they're not prepared for in a country which doesn't see fit to set up any system to help when the marriage breaks down.'

'But you can't have people going into marriages knowing they can get out of them.' Pat was very familiar with the argument from fourth-year debating clubs at school.

'Well, you certainly can't go into a marriage, a doubtful marriage, knowing you can't get out of it,' Cathy had said.

She had gone to London. five days later. Everyone else had been told that she was doing this wonderful new post-graduate course. It was a special qualification in EEC law; it was obviously the absolutely necessary qualification of the future. Mum had said that with all the changes that were going to come about from Brussels and Strasbourg and everything, Cathy was doing the right thing. Pat knew that Cathy would not come back. She knew that the family had broken up, and broken much more permanently than when Ethna had gone to be a nun. Ethna hadn't really left at all, even though she was in Australia: Cathy was only an hour away but she had gone for ever.

Ethna had never been told why Cathy had gone to England. At Christmas the long letter with the small slanted writing had wanted to know all about the course that Cathy was doing and what her address was and what holidays she would get for the Christmas festivities. Nobody wrote and told Ethna that Cathy hadn't come home for Christmas. Perhaps Cathy had written, but it was certainly never mentioned in the weekly letters which came and went; every week a green Irish air letter on the hall table begun by Mum, where Dad and Pat added bits; and every week, but slightly out of synch, a blue air letter from Australia with details of Sister this who had done that and Sister that who had done this. And all of the time nothing from Cathy.

At about the time that Cathy's baby should be born Pat had asked Mum for the address. 'I wanted to write and see if there was anything we could do.'

'Oh, there's nothing any of *us* could do,' Mum had said bitterly. 'If there had been anything then we would have been glad to do it, but no, we knew nothing, your sister knew everything. So she knew best and went off on her own. No, I don't think there's anything *we* could do. I don't think it would be welcomed.'

'But, Mum, it's your grandchild. Your own grandchild.' Pat had been almost seventeen and full of outrage.

'Yes, and Ian's mother, Mrs Kennedy, it's her first grandchild too. But are either of us being allowed the privilege of having a grandchild, and a baby we all want, and a christening, and a fuss, and the birthright of any child? No, no, a lot of claptrap about not wanting to settle down and not wanting to be tied down. I wonder does Miss Cathy ever ask herself where she would be if I had felt that way?' Mum had got very pink in the face about it.

'I'm sure she's very grateful to you, Mum.'

'Oh I'm sure she is, very sure. Yes, she must be. Fine life *she'd* have had if she had been given away to an adoption society the moment she saw the light of day because I couldn't be tied down.'

'But you were married already, Mum, and you did have Ethna.'

'That's not the *point*,' Mum had roared.

And suddenly Pat had realised what had been said.

'Is Cathy giving the baby away, she can't be giving the baby away, can she?'

'I'm not permitted to know what she's doing. We're not in her confidence, your father and I, but I *assume* that's what she's doing. If she can't be "tied down" to a perfectly reasonable nice boy like Ian Kennedy, then it's very unlikely that she can be tied down to an illegitimate baby which she would have to rear on her own.'

Pat had gone to the firm of solicitors where Ian Kennedy worked with his father. He was a nice, red-haired boy, about the friendliest of all Cathy's boy friends; it was a pity she hadn't married him.

'I came to talk to you about Cathy,' she had said.

'Yeah, great, how is she?' he had asked.

'I think she's fine . . . ' Pat had been nonplussed.

'Good, give her my love when you write, will you?'

'I don't have her address, and Mum is being difficult. You know, not being able to lay her hands on it . . . '

'Oh, I don't know where she is now,' said Ian.

'Doesn't she keep in touch?' Pat was shocked again.

'No, she said she didn't want to. Said she wanted to be free.'

'But . . . ?'

'But what?'

'Doesn't she keep you informed . . . let you know . ?'

'Know what?'

Pat paused. Now, it had been definitely said, definitely, about six months ago, that Ian had been told of her decision to go to England on account of the pregnancy. Yes, Ian had even been in the house. He had said to Dad that he was very happy indeed to acknowledge that he was responsible for the child, and to marry Cathy if she would have him. Pat knew that he had said he wanted to support the child, and to see it when it was born; he couldn't have forgotten about all that, could he?

'I'm sorry for being silly,' Pat had said. 'I'm the baby of the family and nobody tells me anything.'

'Yes?' Ian smiled kindly.

'But I thought she'd be having the, er, baby, now and I wanted to know how she was . . . that's why I'm here.'

'But didn't she tell you? She must have told you?' Ian's face was lined with concern.

'What? Told me what?'

'It was a false alarm — she wasn't pregnant at all.'

'I don't believe you.'

'Of course! Hey, you must know this. She wrote and told everyone just after she went to London.'

'It's not true . . . '

'Of course it's true. She wrote and told us all. It was a very early test she had here, not a proper one.'

'So why didn't she come back?'

'What?'

'If it was a false alarm why didn't she come back to her job and home and to you and everything?'

'Oh, Pat, you *know* all this . . . she was a bit peeved with your Mum and Dad. She thought there'd be more solidarity, I think. And she was very pissed off with me.'

'Why was she pissed off with you? You said you'd marry her.'

'But that's not what she wanted, she wanted . . . oh, I don't know . . . anyway, it wasn't necessary.'

'So why isn't she back?'

'As I said, we all let her down. She was annoyed. She wrote, when she told me about the false alarm bit, and said she didn't feel like coming back. She must have written to your family too. Of course she did.'

'She didn't,' Pat said definitely.

'But whyever not? Why didn't she put them out of their agony?'

'*Their* agony?'

'You know what I mean. It's an expression.'

'She never wrote.'

'Oh Pat, nonsense, of course she did. Maybe they didn't tell you. You said yourself they kept things from you.'

'They don't know it was a false alarm, I know that much.'

She said goodbye to Ian, and she promised she

wouldn't make a lot of trouble for everyone, she'd be a good little girl.

'You're a real *enfant terrible*, you know. You're much too grown-up and pretty to be playing that Saint Trinian's kind of thing.'

She put out her tongue at him, and they both laughed.

*   *   *

Mum said she didn't want to discuss Cathy. Cathy had found nothing to discuss with her, why should she spend time talking about Cathy?

'But Ian says he heard from her as soon as she went. It was all a false alarm, she never had a baby, she was never pregnant at all. Aren't you pleased now, isn't that good news, Mum?' Pat pleaded with her.

'That's as may be,' Mum had said.

*   *   *

Just as she was dropping off to sleep that night, Pat thought of something that made her sit up again, wide-awake.

Now she knew why Mum hadn't been pleased. Cathy must have had an abortion. That's why there was no baby, that's why Cathy had not come back. But why hadn't she told Ian? Or Mum? And mainly why hadn't she come back?

*   *   *

'Do you think the other nuns read Ethna's letters?' Pat had asked a few days later when the green aerogramme was being sealed up and sent off.

'Very unlikely,' Dad had said.

'It's not the dark ages. They don't censor their correspondence,' Mum had said.

'Anyway she can be fairly critical of some of the other nuns; she gives that Sister Kevin a hard time,' Dad said. 'I don't expect she'd do that if they read her outgoing letters anyway.'

Pat thought that it was nice that Dad read Ethna's letters so carefully that he knew which sister was which.

*   *   *

Pat had written to Ethna; first of all a probing letter. 'I'm getting older and a bit, though not much, wiser. One of the things that upsets me is the cloak of silence that hangs over Cathy, and where she is in England and what she's doing and what the situation is. Could you tell me what the situation is as far as you know it and then I'll take it from there . . . '

She had a letter from Ethna, not on an aerogramme but in an envelope. On the outside of the envelope it said, 'The Stamps You Wanted'. That satisfied any curiosity Mum and Dad might have had. Inside it was very short.

'I really think you are making a mystery about nothing. Poor Cathy has been punished quite enough, she thought that she was indeed going to have a child. And since she was not at all willing or ready to marry the father then it is merciful that this was not so. She is happy in London, where she is doing social work. She has hardened her heart to mother and father, which is a great pity, but in time I am sure she will feel ready to open up doors of friendship again. She doesn't write to me, apart from that one letter which told me all these things; since nobody has ever mentioned anything to me about it in letters from home, I have never mentioned anything either. I pray for her, and I pray for all of you. Life is so short, it seems sad that any of it should be spent in feeling a grievance and a hurt when a hand held out would brush all the unhappiness away.'

Great help, Pat had thought at the time; punished enough, hardened her heart, brush all the unhappiness away; nun's phrases, and not a word of blame about Mum and Dad who were always writing letters to the paper protesting about letting South African rugby teams into the country. They were always talking about itinerants, and they had raised money for refugees. Why were they so hard-hearted about Cathy?

Pat had decided that she was not going to allow Cathy to disappear without trace as if some terrible crime or shame had settled on the family and people hoped that by ignoring it things would return to normal. She had tackled them at supper the night she had got Ethna's letter.

'This family is becoming a bit like nine green bottles,' she said.

'What on earth do you mean?' Dad was smiling.

'First Ethna goes off to the other side of the world, and then we are four. Then six months ago Cathy disappears without trace and now we are three. Will I go off somewhere too?'

Dad was still smiling but he looked puzzled. He stood up to fetch the coffee percolator. He looked tired and a bit beaten. Not the cheerful doctor, always in a smart suit, always optimistic, always seeing the best for patients and neighbours alike. He wore his cardigan at home, and Mum wore an old jumper that was torn under the arms. They looked shabby and a bit dishevelled as they sat in the big dining room with its good furniture and its expensive cut glass decanters. Pat felt that somehow they didn't make any effort when it was only just her. She was sure they had been far more elegant and lively when Ethna was at home and when Cathy was there.

'Are you just waiting for me to go off and that will be the hat trick?'

'What is this, Pat, what silly game are you playing?' Mum was not very amused.

'No, I mean it, Mum. It's not much of a family, is it?'

'Don't speak to your mother like that.' Dad was surprised and hurt. He had thought that talking about green bottles was going to be a joke; now it had turned into a row.

'It's not normal. People marry and have children, they don't have them just to export them off as fast as possible.'

Mum was very annoyed indeed. 'Ethna was twenty-one when she left. She had wanted to join this order for two years. Do you think we wanted Ethna to go to that outlandish place? Or to be a nun at all? Don't be so ridiculous, and have some thought for other people before you start your hurtful accusations.'

'No, I know that's Ethna, but then Cathy's gone. This house used to be full of people, now it's just us. And soon I suppose you'll want me to go. Would you prefer if I tried to get into UCC or Galway or maybe England rather than Belfield, then you wouldn't have to have me around the place and you could be all on your own?' She stood up, tears in her eyes.

'Apologise this minute to your mother, this minute, do you hear me!'

'Why to Mum? I'm saying it to both of you.'

She was about to leave the room when Mum had said wearily, 'Come back, Pat. Come back and I'll talk to you about Cathy.'

'You owe her no explanation, Peggy, none, not after the way she's spoken to you.' Dad's face was red with disappointment.

'Sit down, Pat. Please.' Grudgingly and shrugging, Pat sat down.

'I'm not going to fight with you. I'm going to agree with you. It's not much of a family, it certainly isn't. When your father and I got married this is not what we had in mind at all.'

'Now Peg, now Peg,' Dad said warningly.

'No, the girl is right to question what's happened. We question it ourselves, for God's sake. Not at all what we had in mind. I suppose we had in mind the practice getting bigger and going well. It has. That's all fine, that side of it. And we had in mind our friends and all the people we like being around, and that's gone well. And our health has been fine. But mainly what we had in mind was the three of you. That's what people do have in mind actually, Pat, that's what they have in mind most of the day and night when they have children. From the time that Ethna was here we've had you three in mind more than anything else.'

Pat gave a very slight shrug. It was a disclaimer. It was meant to say, you don't have to tell me all this. I know you tried. As a shrug it worked. Mum had known what she meant.

'I know you think I'm just saying this to be nice to you, or maybe perhaps that we started out with good intentions and lost them on the way. But it wasn't like that. I think some of my best times, and yours,

Hugh, were when Ethna was about six or seven, and Cathy was five, and you were a baby. Three little girls totally dependent on us, all lighting up with enthusiasm . . . '

'Sure Mum. Yes. Sure.'

'No, give me a very short minute for the sentimental sugary bit because it didn't last long. Then you were all so bright. This was another joy, some of our friends had problems. Well, we didn't call them problems but so and so's child couldn't read until he was seven, or someone couldn't settle at school, or another wouldn't manage to get on with the teachers, or failed the third Honours in her leaving. Not you three, from Ethna on we knew, top of the class, exams no real problem. Do you remember Ethna's conferring?'

'Yes . . . I got the day off school.'

'And she looked so bright . . . that's a funny word, but she did, you know, clear eyes and alert face, compared to a lot of the others. I thought, ours is very bright, there's so much before her when she gets this ridiculous nunnish thing out of her system . . . '

'But I thought you approved?'

'We had to approve in the end.' Dad spoke for the first time. 'Of course we didn't approve. Use your head, Pat, suppose you had brought up a lovely girl like Ethna, as bright as a button as Mum says, who has just got a First class honours degree in history and who wants to go with a crowd of half-educated women to a school in the outback of somewhere because she read a book about the damn place and she met a recruiting team!'

'But you never said. I don't remember . . . '

'You don't remember. How old were you — twelve, thirteen? What discussions could we have had with you about it that would have helped anything except add to the argument?'

Mum had interrupted. 'We didn't even discuss it with Cathy because we didn't want gangs forming and pressure being put on Ethna. We just talked to her.'

'And what did you want her to do?' Pat wanted to know.

'I'd have liked her to do an M.A. and then a doctorate. She was very, very good. I spoke to some of the people in there, they said she had the makings of a scholar, and I'd have liked her to have had a good lively life here, instead of putting up with Sister Kevin's tantrums in a jungle.' Dad had sounded very defeated when he said that, as if remembering the whole battle and how it was lost.

'Yes, that's what I'd have liked too. I'd have liked her to go on living here, it was so near and handy, and got a small car and had friends and gone off to the West for weekends. And then married someone in her own field, some professor, and got a house near by and I could have seen the whole thing over again with her children, growing up and learning to walk . . . '

'It's a fairly normal, reasonable wish, isn't it?' Dad had asked defensively. 'Rather than see a whole life, a whole education, and talent, thrown away.'

'She's happy though, she says she is,' Mum had said.

'I suppose her letters to us are about as near the truth as ours are to her,' Dad had said. And there was a silence as they thought about the implications of that.

'So Cathy . . . ?' Pat spoke softly, hoping that the mood hadn't been broken, that she could still get her mother to talk.

'Cathy,' Mum had said.

'Cathy was no trouble either. Everyone else told us of all their sleepless nights over their terrible teenage children. We never had any,' Dad smiled at Pat as if he was thanking her. She felt a twinge of guilt.

'And Cathy did have her friends around much more than Ethna, and they used to laugh, and they were full of life. Do you remember the summer they did the whole garden, Hugh?'

Dad had laughed. 'All I had to do was provide one of those big cans of beer at the end of the day. They dug and they weeded and they cut hedges and grass.'

'It never looked back since,' Mum had said. 'It used to be a wilderness and they tamed it.'

'All for a few cans of beer,' Dad had said. They stopped talking for a moment. Pat said nothing.

'So Cathy was going to be the one who might be with us, when Ethna went. It wasn't a transfer of love. I suppose it was changing the plans or hopes. And she was so enthusiastic, about everything.'

'We felt we were qualifying with her, she was so entertaining about it all — the lectures, the course, the solicitors' exams down in the Four Courts, the apprenticeship . . it was all so alive,' Dad had said.

'And she seemed to get on so well with Ian. I kept thinking, she's only twenty-two, she's far too young to settle down but then of course I told myself I was only twenty-two when I married. Then on the other hand, I didn't have a career to decide about. Then I went back to the first hand and said since Ian and Cathy were both solicitors and Ian's father had a firm, well then, surely if they did have a couple of children and she wanted to work part-time it couldn't be too hard to arrange.'

Dad had interrupted. 'This is what your mother meant about you children always being in our minds. We had Cathy married to Ian in our minds long before they even kissed each other.'

'But why couldn't you accept Cathy's decision like you did for Ethna? You didn't want Ethna to go off and be a nun but when she did you sort of acknowledged it.'

'Yes,' Mum had said, 'Yes, it made her so happy and it was her life. Much as I wanted to I couldn't control it any more . . . she had to do what she wanted.'

'So why couldn't Cathy do what she wanted?'

'That was different.'

'But why, Mum, why? It's not as if you and Dad were prudes or anything, it's not as if your friends would cut you off, or as if you'd be ashamed to lift your heads. Why can't Cathy bring her baby home?'

'It's different,' Dad had said.

'I can't think why, I really can't. Nobody minds. Ian doesn't mind. I talked to him. He's very casual about Cathy — "send her my love" he said. Ethna won't mind. I wrote to her about it, but, but . . .'

'You wrote to Ethna?' Mum had said, surprised.

'Yes, to try and clear things up.'

'And did it?'

'No, not at all.'

'What did you want cleared up?' Dad had asked.

'Whether Cathy is having a baby or is not. Something very basic and simple like that, which most normal families would know.'

Dad had looked at Mum, and she had said, 'Tell her.'

'The answer is . . . that we don't know.'

'You don't *know*?'

'No. That's the truth.' Mum had continued, 'We were very shocked by Cathy's attitude. She was very harshly critical of us, and the way we lived, and thought that our attitudes were hypocritical, you know, to preach some kind of broadmindedness and then not to follow it.'

'But we didn't see it like that. You see, it was nothing to do with acceptance or reputations, we thought Cathy was being silly and making extravagant gestures, turning herself into a Protest just for the sake of it. "Look at me, I'm too modern to do like anyone else, give my child a name and a home and a background, no, I'm far too sophisticated for that!" We didn't like it, Pat, it was too studenty . . . '

'There's no need to go over all that was said, you probably heard most of it, but to cut a long story short we have only heard from Cathy once since she went to London. I always imply — well, let's be honest, I always tell people lies and say that we've heard from her, but she wrote only once two weeks after she left.'

'Did she say . . . ?'

'She said that it had been a false alarm, that her dates had been wrong, that she was only a shorter time overdue than she thought and that everything was fine.'

There was a silence.

'And did you believe her, Mum?'

'No.'

'Did you, Dad?'

'No. I didn't.'

'It was too far for there to be a mistake?'

'Well, she said she had left a specimen into Holles Street and they had said it was positive. They don't make mistakes.'

'But she says they did.'

'No, she's forgotten she told us that bit, I think.'

'Oh.'

'So we know no more than you do,' Mum had said, spreading out her hands helplessly.

'But why do you say everything's all right . . . ?'

'Because it will be one way or another, sometime, and we don't want Cathy to have to walk back into a whole lot of complications. Keep it simple, is our motto.'

'So what do you believe if you don't believe what Cathy said?'

'Well, what do you think?'

'No, what do you think?'

'Pat, either she had a termination or she is in fact having the child, and as you so rightly pointed out to me, if she is having the baby it's due this month.'

'And we don't know?'

'We don't know.'

'We don't even know where she is?'

'No.'

Then Mum had started to cry, and she cried with her arms down on the table and her head on top of them. Right into the dishes and the food. And Dad had stood up and come over and patted her awkwardly on one side and Pat had patted her awkwardly on the other.

'It's all right, Peg,' Dad had said, over and over.

'It's all right, Mum,' Pat had said, over and over.

*   *   *

It had been a hard thing to sit your Leaving Certificate not knowing where your sister was, whether she was alive or dead, and not knowing if you were an aunt

145

or not. But Pat had gone on and done it: she had got all her Honours and plenty of points. Peggy and Hugh's third daughter was on her way to University College, Dublin, registering as a student in Belfield.

Cathy wrote home that year just before Christmas. She said she had seen enough of other people's miseries in her case-load in London to make her realise that most of life's troubles were caused by families. She would like to say very sincerely that she had been entirely to blame for any little fracas they had had. She asked forgiveness and if they liked she would love to come home for Christmas, but since she had been so difficult and stayed out of touch for so long, over a year, she could well understand if they said no. She gave her address for them to reply. It was in Hackney. Mum and Dad had sent a telegram five minutes after the letter arrived. The telegram had read, 'Welcome home, darling Cathy, to the silliest parents and the happiest Christmas ever.'

Cathy had also written to Pat.

'You may well wonder what the Prodigal thinks she's up to, and I don't want to put your nose out of joint. I'll tell you everything you want to know, if you want to know anything, when I see you, and if you have no time for me I'll understand that too. It was utterly selfish of me to go away and leave you as a teenager, in your last year at school, to cope with all the trauma and drama. But when there's a crisis people only think of themselves, or I did anyway. I hope the reunion won't be a damp squib. I haven't kept in touch with most of my friends, so can I ask you to fill the house a bit with people so that we don't become too hot-house and raise our family expectations too high? I'll stop asking and taking soon and start giving, I promise.'

Pat had thought this was very sensible. She asked her College friends in on the evening that Cathy came back. Mum had gone to the airport to meet her and by the time Pat had come home conversation was quite normal. In fact, so normal it was almost frightening. It was as if Cathy had never gone away, as if no mystery hung over the events of the past year. Cathy had said that Pat looked smashing, and that students must be dressing better than in her day, and there wasn't time for much more conversation because they had to get the mulled wine ready, which involved a lot of conversation about what you did to mull it, and how to ensure you didn't boil the alcohol out of it. Pat had been startled to see that they were all laughing quite naturally in the kitchen when Dad had said he should test each batch they made, just in case the flavouring needed adjusting. 'You haven't changed, Dad,' Cathy had laughed, and nobody made any flicker of an eyelid as the moment passed and Cathy's long absence had now sunk into the collective memory. It could be mentioned without being questioned.

It had been like that all that Christmas, and nothing seemed more natural at the end of the holiday than for Cathy to say that she would be coming back for good as soon as she had found a replacement for herself. She was going to work in Ian's office; they had a vacancy in a couple of months. Pat had been puzzled when she saw Cathy and Ian Kennedy strolling around the wintry wilderness of garden, plucking at bushes and pointing out what should be done with hard, frozen-looking flowerbeds. What was going on inside that red head of Ian Kennedy's? Did he not wonder whether Cathy had given birth to his child in London all by herself in

147

a hospital with no friends to come and visit her? Did he not worry about his child, their child, being given to an adoption society and never knowing what it should have known?

Did Ian Kennedy wonder whether Cathy had gone long, long ago to a doctor in England in order to organise a termination of pregnancy and then overnight in one of those nursing homes everyone knew about, where simple minor surgery under anaesthetic would ensure that Cathy and Ian's child didn't ever come into being? Surely he wasn't so foolish as to think that a girl could be pregnant, disappear for over a year and have some vague belief that the pregnancy was all a false alarm.

People were really behaving more and more peculiarly, Pat decided. The older they got the vaguer they became. Ethna's letters now had nice bland welcoming bits about Cathy in them. Had she forgotten all that earlier stuff about punishment, and hardening her heart, and praying for her? Once people got any way settled they seemed to lose touch with reality and built themselves a comfortable little world like a Wendy House entirely of their own creation.

*　　　*　　　*

She had told this to Rory a few times, and he had tried to understand it. But Rory thought that her whole life was a fraud, and that anyone who owned any kind of private house was already out of touch with society. Rory was in her Economics tutorial, by far the most brilliant student of his year, a great thorn in a lot of University flesh. Rory had economic arguments for revolution which could not be faulted.

148

Rory agreed with Pat that the whole Cathy business was very unreal. Rory said he loved Pat, and Pat was very sure that she loved Rory.

*　　　*　　　*

'It's a mistake to get too involved with anyone your first year in College,' Cathy had said. 'It ties you down, you should have the freedom to roam round and see who you like and who you don't. You should get to know a lot of people, not just sticking together two by two as if you were the animals going into the ark.' Pat didn't like this remark. It was too reminiscent of Cathy saying she couldn't be tied down to marry Ian. It also implied a criticism of Rory. And that was not allowed.

There was nothing that Mum and Dad could find fault with in Rory; they wanted to, but they couldn't actually put a finger on anything. He certainly didn't distract her from her work; in fact he insisted that she work harder than she was prepared to. He said her essays weren't sufficiently researched; he lent her books, he came with her to the library and sat opposite her. It was easier to do the damn stuff than to find excuses. He didn't keep her out at all night parties. He had explained to Mum and Dad that he didn't drink much so there wouldn't be any danger of drunken driving late at night in his little beat-up car. When they went away to conferences or student festivals in Cork or Galway, Rory always managed to drop the one phrase which would reassure Mum and Dad about the set-up. 'I'll leave Pat at the girls' house first and then she can settle in and I'll go off and find where they're putting the lads up . . . ' Some trivial little remark which would prevent Mum and Dad from wondering what exactly the score was.

The score was exactly as Rory described it for a long time.

'I suppose you think it's silly not to,' Pat had said.

'Silly, no. Wasteful, yes,' Rory had said. 'It's up to you entirely what you would like to do. I don't ever believe in putting on the pressure. Too much of what's wrong is wrong because people felt forced to do things for approval. But I think you're wrong. It would give us both so much pleasure and it would hurt exactly nobody. We aren't betraying anyone, we can be sure that we aren't irresponsibly conceiving a child we don't want. So wasteful is all I think I'd say it was.'

She adored Rory, his intensity and his boyish enthusiasms. She went to the Family Planning Clinic. She knew the doctor who was on duty that day. It was a friend of her father's. 'Glad to see you, that's a good sensible girl,' the friend of Dad's had said. No explanations asked for, no curiosity, no condemnation. It was all so simple. Why hadn't Cathy done this? They had clinics, even in her time.

Cathy was still a mystery. There she was, living at home so calmly. If anyone ever asked about the Common Market Legal course she was meant to have done, she would shake her head and say that she hadn't done it after all, she had worked for the Council in East London. Mum had been right in her way to have kept things simple, to have rocked no boats. Cathy came back and stepped in more or less where she had got out. It was just that time, all those months that remained as inexplicable. What had she been doing, what had she been thinking? She was so placid now, sometimes going out to the theatre with Ian, sometimes with other people. Holidaying with two girls in the Greek islands, sitting with Mum and Dad sometimes in the evenings looking at television.

Pat had insisted on Rory discussing it. 'Is it natural for them not to mention it? Is it normal? I mean, there she is at home, and nobody ever once refers to the fact that she left home pregnant and stayed away from home for fourteen months and came back and everything is as you were.'

'Um.' Rory was reading.

'But why, why do they say nothing? It's like not noticing someone is naked or not referring to someone being in a car crash or in gaol. It's not real.'

'Um. I know,' he said.

'But they don't seem to want to know, it's only me, it's only me that wants to know.'

'Well, why don't you ask her then?' Rory said.

*　　　　*　　　　*

'Cathy, did you have any problems with the Pill, you know, have you had to change brand or anything?'

Cathy looked up from the papers she was studying. She was sitting at the big desk in her bedroom, which she had converted into a kind of study.

'No, I was never on the Pill, so it didn't occur.'

'Never on the Pill, at all?'

'No.'

'How amazing.'

'Pat, you are twenty, going on twenty-one. You aren't actually a wise old sociologist commenting on the funny things society does.' Cathy laughed good-naturedly as she spoke.

'Yes, but . . . not ever?'

'Not ever. If I *had* been, that little incident which

you may remember would never have happened . . .'

'Yes, well, after the little incident . . . ?'

Pat felt she was treading on a minefield. She had to remain light-hearted and casual.

'Oh, after the little incident, I didn't . . . how shall I put it . . . well, I didn't actually need the services of a contraceptive.'

'Not ever?'

'No, not ever.' Cathy smiled, relaxed and calm as if they had been talking about the replanting of the herbaceous border.

'Oh.'

'So I'm not much help. But you could go to the Family Planning Clinic, tell them if it doesn't suit you. They'll change it.'

'Yes, good idea. Cathy?'

'Yes?'

'Remember that time . . . the little incident . . . what happened?'

'How do you mean, what happened?'

'I mean, did you go through with it? Did you have the baby?'

'Did I what?'

'Did you have the baby? In London?'

'Hey, what is this? A joke?'

'No, seriously. I wish you'd tell me. I hate us all pretending, it's so artificial.'

'Tell you what?'

'When you went off to London, did you actually have the baby?'

'No, of course I didn't, are you feeling all right? What an extraordinary question to ask. Have a baby? Where is it, then, if I had it, was I meant to have left it in a telephone box?'

'Well, what did you do? Did you have an abortion?'

'Seriously, is this some kind of game? Of course I didn't. What on earth are you saying . . . ?'

'But you *were* pregnant.'

'No, I thought I was. I wasn't.'

'You were, Dad knows, he said so when you were gone.'

'Oh no, he can't have, I wrote telling them it was a false alarm.'

'He didn't believe you.'

'Listen, don't start stirring up a lot of trouble over nothing. It was nothing. Why all this interrogation?'

'Is that what put you off the whole thing, fellows and making love?' Pat asked. 'They say people can get very depressed.'

'I *didn't* have an abortion, and I wasn't very heavily into fellows and making love, and I haven't gone off fellows.'

'That's all you'll say.'

'Jesus Lord, what is this, Pat, one of Rory's revolutionary tribunals? You've asked me about ten questions. I've answered all of them honestly — which is rather good of me since *none* of them are any of your business.'

'I'm sorry.'

'No, you're not, you want some awful group where everyone sits and tells the most god-awful, self-centred, boring details of what they did and what they thought and what they felt and what they did then, and what they thought then and what they felt then . . . honestly, I can't stand that kind of thing. Even Woody Allen laughs at it, for heaven's sake. It's not going to solve the world's problems.'

'What is?'

'I don't know, but a lot of people's are solved by playing down dramas rather than creating them.'

'And is that what you're doing?'

'I'm refusing to invent them, refusing to make myself into a tragedy queen.'

'I m sorry I spoke.'

'I'm not, but I'm glad you've stopped.' Cathy grinned.

Pat gave a watery grin back.

*　　*　　*

'So you see, she's *got* to be lying. Somewhere along the line she told a lie.' Pat frowned as she ticked the items off on her fingers.

'There are times you can be very boring, Pat,' said Rory.

She was hurt and upset. 'You're often analysing what people say and why society forces us to tell lies and role-play. Why is it boring when I do it?'

'Because it's repetitive and it's slapdash.'

'How do you mean?'

'Well, you haven't even included all the possibilities, have you?'

'I *have*. Either she was not pregnant, or she was and she had either a baby or an abortion.'

'She could have had a miscarriage, you clown.'

*　　*　　*

All that had been a year ago. Pat remembered the conversation word for word. They had been all at the turning points of things somehow. The very next day, the day following the interrogation, Cathy said that she and Ian were going to get married. The news coincided with a letter from Ethna. She was leaving the order. And everyone might remember that she had spoken quite a lot of Father Fergus. Well, Fergus was in Rome at the moment and the laicisation process was well under way. She and Fergus would be married in Rome during the summer. Then they would come home, possibly try to get a teaching job. It shouldn't be hard. Both of them had a lot of qualifications and a lot of experience.

'It's all working out as you want, isn't it, Mum?' Pat had said.

'It's what all you girls want that's important, you know that,' Mum had said; she was laughing at herself a little, and she tried to take the triumphant look off her face.

That time had been a turning point for Pat too. Rory had told her about the South American woman, Cellina. Pat had liked Cellina; she had helped her to organise a solidarity campaign for fellow students back home, and she had introduced her to Rory. She had been pleased when Rory had liked Cellina. She had never seen exactly how much he had liked Cellina until he told her.

She had stopped taking the Pill. To use Cathy's marvellous, old-fashioned phrase, she felt she didn't need the services of a contraceptive. She did a lot of work on her thesis, and she did a great deal of work at home too. A family wedding for Cathy, with the Kennedys screaming their delight as loudly as Mum and Dad. Then there was the trip to Rome. Why not? If Ethna was doing something as huge as this they must all be there, and they were. Mother had Ethna back, and she had Cathy back.

But she was about to lose Pat. Temporarily perhaps, who could tell? Rory had come back from Bonn where he and Cellina had been living. He had come home alone. They had met a lot during the two weeks he was back. It seemed silly and wasteful not to go to bed with him. They were giving each other a lot of pleasure and they weren't hurting anyone, since Cellina would never know. And were they betraying anyone? The word betrayal is such a subjective one.

But now Rory had gone back to Bonn, and Holles Street, which is never wrong over such things, had said Positive. And Pat had learned enough over the years not to believe the Problem Pages. It would be best if she went to London, on her own. Connected with work. And the possibility of getting into the London School of Economics — yes, that would be a good one. She had often spoken of the LSE. Mum and Dad would be interested in that as a project.

And as long as she wrote regularly and seemed happy, that was the main thing.

Seven people woke up that morning and remembered that this was the day Gerry Moore came out of the nursing home. He wouldn't be cured, of course. You were never cured if you were an alcoholic. Four of them shrugged and thought that perhaps he wasn't really an alcoholic — these things were so exaggerated nowadays. There was a time when a man took a drop too much, but now it was all endogynous, and in the glands, and in the bloodstream, and there were allergies and addictions that had never existed before. Two people knew very well that he was an alcoholic, and the remaining one, waking up that morning, looking forward to his release, had never believed for one moment that there was anything the matter with Gerry. He had gone into that home for a good rest, and that's all there was to it.

*　　*　　*

Gerry's mother was seventy-three, and there had never been any scandal in her life before and there wasn't going to be any. She had reared five boys on her own. Three of them were abroad now, all of them making a good living; only two were in Ireland, and of those Gerry was easily her favourite. A big innocent bear of a man without a screed of harm in him. He worked too hard, that was the problem and in his job, Gerry had told her often, the best place to meet clients was in pubs. A grown man couldn't sit like a baby in a pub, drinking a pint of orange juice! Naturally a man had to drink with the people he talked to. They wouldn't trust him otherwise. His health had broken down from all the anti-social hours, that's what he had told her. He had to go into the nursing home for six weeks for a total rest. No one was to come and see him. He would be out in the first week of May, he had said. Now it was the beginning of May and he'd be home, as right as rain. That's if anyone could be as right as rain in the house his precious Emma ran for him. Stop. She mustn't say a word against Emma, everyone thought Emma was the greatest thing since sliced bread. Keep your own counsel about Emma. Even her son Jack had said that Emma was a walking saint. Jack! Who never noticed anyone . . .

*　　*　　*

Jack Moore woke up that morning with a leaden feeling in his chest. He couldn't identify it for a while. He went through the things that might cause it. No, he had no row going on with Mr. Power in the showrooms; no, he had no great bag of washing to take down to the launderette. No, there had been no bill from the garage for his car — and then he remembered. Gerry came home today. Insisted on taking a bus home in his own time, no, he didn't want anyone to collect him, didn't want to look like a wheelchair case. Anyway, he had to start taking control of his own life again. Jack knew that the visit to the

158

nursing home was going to be a big talking point, a drama, a bit of glamour, just like losing his driving licence had been. Gerry had held them spellbound with his story of the young guard asking him to blow into the bag. The jokes that Gerry had made had cracked a smile even in the Gardai. It hadn't done any good in the end, of course, he had been put off the roads for a year. Emma had taken twenty-five driving lessons in ten days: she had passed her test. She drove the car, remembering to take the keys out of it when she was going to leave both the car and Gerry at home. Emma was a saint, a pure saint. He hoped her children appreciated her.

*   *   *

Paul and Helen Moore woke up and remembered that this was the day that Daddy came home. They were a lot more silent at breakfast than usual. Their mother had to remind them of the good news. When they got back from school their Dad would be sitting at home as cured from his disease as he could hope to be. Their faces were solemn. But they should be cheerful, their mother told them, everything was going to be fine now. Dad had gone of his own choice into a place where they gave him tests and rest and therapy. Now he knew that drinking alcohol for him was like drinking poison, and he wouldn't do it. Paul Moore was fourteen. He had been going to go and play in his friend Andy's house after school, but that wouldn't be a good idea now. Not if a cured father was coming back. He never asked his friends to play in their house. Well. It was only one day. Helen Moore was twelve; she wished that her mother didn't go *on* about things so much, with that kind of false,

bright smile. It was better really to be like Father
Vincent who said that the Lord arranged things the
way the Lord knew best. Father Vincent believed
that the Lord thought it was best for Dad to be drunk
most of the time. Or that's what it seemed that
Father Vincent thought. He was never too definite
about anything.

*   *   *

Father Vincent woke wishing that Gerry Moore
had a face that was easier to read. He had been to see
him six times during his cure. Gerry had ended up the
most cheerful patient in the nursing home; he had
nurses, nuns and other patients agog with his stories
of the people he had photographed, the adventures,
the mistakes corrected just in time, the disasters
miraculously averted. Alone with the priest, he had
put on a serious face the way other people put on a
raincoat, temporarily, not regarding it as anything to
be worn in real life. Yes, Gerry had understood the
nature of his illness, and wasn't it bad luck — a hell
of a lot of other fellows could drink what he drank
and get off scot free. But he would have to give it
up. Heigh Ho. But then the priest had heard him
tell stories about photographing film stars on
location, and meeting famous people face to face.
Nowhere did he seem to remember that he hadn't
done a book for four years, nor a proper commission
for two. He had spent most of his time drinking with
that friend of his from RTE, the fellow who was
apparently able to get his work finished by twelve
noon and spend the rest of the day in Madigans. A
hard man, poor Gerry used to call him. Des the hard
man. Father Vincent hoped that Des-the-hard-man

would be some help when Gerry got out of all this. But he doubted it. Des didn't look like a pillar for anyone to lean on.

*   *   *

Des Kelly woke up at five a.m. as he always did. He slipped out of the bed so as not to wake Clare: he had become quite an expert at it over the years. He kept his clothes in a cupboard on the stairs so that he could dress in the bathroom without disturbing her. In half an hour he was washed, dressed and had eaten his cornflakes; he took his coffee into his study and lit the first cigarette of the day. God, it was great that Gerry was being let out of that place at last, the poor divil would be glad to be out. He'd been up once to see him and he'd known half the crowd in the sitting room, or half-known them. Gerry wasn't well that day, so he'd scribbled a note to say he'd called. He'd felt so helpless, since his automatic response had been to leave a bottle of whiskey. Still, it was all over now, and no harm done. Pumped all the poison out of him they had, told him to lay off it for a bit longer, then go easy on it. Or that's what Des supposed they told him, that made sense anyway. If you got as reached by the stuff as poor old Gerry had been getting there over the last few months, it was wiser to call a halt for a bit. What he couldn't stand was all this sancti- monious claptrap about it being an illness. There was no fitter man in Dublin than Gerry Moore. He had been a bit unfortunate. But now he had time to take stock and get his career together, well, he'd be back on top in no time. That's if Know-all Emma, you- name-it-I'm-a-specialist-in-it Emma, didn't take con- trol of him and crush any bit of life that was left in him right out of him. Gerry would need to watch it: with a friend like that creeping Jesus Father Vincent, with a coffin-face of a brother like Jack and with know-all Emma for a wife, poor Gerry needed a couple of real friends. One of the few things he and Clare ever saw eye to eye about these days was what a mystery it was that a grand fellow like Gerry Moore had married that Emma. Des sighed at the puzzle of it all and opened his file: he always got his best work done at this time of the morning.

*   *   *

Emma woke up late. She had hardly slept during the night but had fallen into one of those heavy sleeps at dawn. She was sorry now that she hadn't got up at six o'clock when she was so restless; the extra three hours weren't worth it. She tumbled out of bed and went to the handbasin. She gave herself what her mother had called a lick and a promise. She smiled at the way she had accepted the phrase for so long and never questioned it until today. Today of all days she was up late and examining her face in the mirror musing over what old childhood sayings might mean. She pulled on her pale blue sweater and jeans and ran downstairs. Paul and Helen looked at her as reproachfully as if she had handed them over to Dr Barnardo's.

'We had to get our own breakfast,' said Helen.

'You'll be late for work,' said Paul.

'The place looks awful for Daddy coming home,' said Helen.

With her lip well bitten in to stop her shouting at them Emma managed a sort of smile. They had managed to spill water, cold and hot, all over the kitchen. God almighty, it's not that hard to fill an electric kettle and then to pour hot water into cups of instant coffee, is it? She didn't say it, she didn't ask the rhetorical question which would result in shrugging and counter-accusation. They had trailed coffee powder, buttered the sink as well their bread, there was a line of crumbs from the toaster . . . calm, calm.

'Right, if you've had your breakfast, you head off, and we'll have a celebration supper tonight. Isn't it marvellous?' She looked brightly from one to another.

'Why didn't you get up in time, Mummy, if it's such a marvellous day?' Helen asked. Emma felt that she would like to slap her hard.

'I was awake most of the night and I fell into one of those heavy sleeps just a short time ago. Come on now, hoosh, you should be gone . . . .'

'Will the celebration supper last long? Can I go over to Andy's afterwards?'

'Yes!' snapped Emma. 'When supper's over you can do what you like.'

'Is Father Vincent coming to supper?' Helen asked.

'Heavens, no. I mean who would have asked him, why do you think he might be here?' Emma sounded alarmed.

'Because he's often here when there's a crisis, isn't he?'

'But this isn't a crisis. This is the end of the crisis, Daddy is cured, I tell you, cured. All the awful things about his disease are gone, there's no need for Father Vincent to come and be helpful.'

'You don't like Father Vincent much, do you?' said Helen.

'Of course I do, I like him very much, I don't know where you got that idea. It's just that he's not needed tonight.' Emma was wiping and cleaning and scooping things into the sink as she spoke.

'Would you say you like Father Vincent less or more than you like Dad's friend Mr Kelly?'

Emma put her hands on her hips. 'Right, is there anything else you'd like to do before you go to school? Play I Spy? Maybe we could have a few games of charades as well or get out the Monopoly? Will you get yourselves . . . '

They laughed and ran off. She ate the crusts of their toast, rinsed the cups and plates and ran from the kitchen into the sitting room. The children had been right, it was a mess. She took a deep breath and made a big decision. One hour would make all the difference. Please God, may she get someone who was understanding and nice, someone who realised that she wasn't a shirker.

'Hallo, is that RTE? Can you put me through to . . . .' No, suddenly she hung up. It was bad enough having one in the family who let people down: she had never missed a day since she had got the secretarial job in Montrose, she was damned if she was going to miss even an hour today. She swept up the worst of the untidiness, shoving newspapers and magazines into the cupboard, gathering any remaining cups or glasses from last night. Gerry wasn't one to notice what a place looked like.

She threw out the worst of the flowers and changed the water in the vase; then she took out her Welcome Home card and wrote 'from all of us with love.' She propped it up beside the flowers, ran out pulling the door, leapt on her bicycle and headed for Montrose. Because she was a little later than usual there was more traffic, but she didn't mind, she thought of it as a contest. She would fight the cars and the traffic lights and the bits that were uphill. She would think about nice things, like how she had lost a stone and a half in two months, how she could fit into jeans again, how someone had really and truly thought she was a young woman, not the forty-year-old mother of teenagers. She thought of the great sun-tan she would get in the summer; she thought that she might get highlights in her hair if it weren't too dear. She thought of everything in the world except her husband Gerry Moore.

*   *   *

Gerry Moore was going to be a great loss in the nursing home. The nurses all told him that and so did the patients. The doctor had his last chat with him that morning and said that in many ways he had been one of the most successful patients who had ever done the programme because he had refused to let it depress him.

'You've been in such good form all the time, Gerry, you've actually helped other people. I must admit at the start I was less than convinced. I thought you were just marking time to get out and get at the stuff again.'

'Wouldn't I have to be half mad to do that?' Gerry said. The doctor said nothing.

'I know, I know, a lot of the lads you get in here are half mad. But not me. Honestly, I know what I'm doing now. I just have to change my lifestyle, that's all. It can be done. I once had a lifestyle, a grand lifestyle, without drink. I'll have one again.'

'You'll be in here lecturing to us yet,' the doctor laughed.

Gerry had a dozen people to say goodbye to: he

promised he'd come back to see them. 'They all say that,' people said, yet people believed that Gerry Moore would, he had that sort of way with him.

Nurse Dillon said she was surprised that a man like Mr Moore with so many friends of his own didn't want anyone to come and collect him. Gerry had put his arm around her shoulder as she walked him to the door.

'Listen here to me, I'm thinner, I'm much more handsome, I'm a sane man, not a madman. I'm a great fellow now compared to the way I was when I walked in -- so don't you think I should go home my own route and let the world have a look at me?'

She waved at him all the way to the end of the avenue. He was a gorgeous man, Mr Moore, and actually he was right, he did look fabulous now. You'd never think he was an old man of forty-five.

'Mind yourself as you go your own route,' she called.

*   *   *

His own route. Now where would that have taken him in the old days? Stop remembering, stop glorifying . . . a taste was only a taste, it wasn't anything special. He knew that. Stop glamourising it all. These pubs, the ones he might have dropped into, they weren't welcoming corners where friends called him to join their circles; some of them were sordid and depressing. If ever he had got talking to anyone it had been a sour depressed man who might have looked at him with suspicion. It was only when he got back nearer home that he would find people he knew in pubs. Friends. Stop glorifying it. It had *not* been a constant chorus of 'There's Gerry, the very

man, come on over here, Gerry, what'll you have?'
No, it hadn't been like that. People had avoided him,
for God's sake, in the last months. He knew that, he
had faced it. People he had known for years. Boy,
was it going to come as a shock to them when they
saw him with his big glass of Slimline Tonic and a
dash of angostura bitters, the non drinkers' cocktail.
Ho, they'd be surprised, never thought old Gerry
Moore had it in him to change his life.

Gerry walked to the bus stop. He had a small overnight case. He hadn't needed much in the hospital,
just his dressing gown and pyjamas and a wash bag,
really, a couple of books and that was it. Why had his
suitcases always been so heavy in the old days? Oh, of
course, booze in case he would ever be caught short,
and gear for work. No more attention to booze
EVER again, but a lot of attention to work. He was
looking forward to spending a good month sorting
himself out and seeing where he was, then another
month sending out mail shots offering specialised
work. By midsummer he should be back where he
had been, only better. A bus came and he got into it.
Happily, he reached into his pocket and got out the
money Emma had brought him. He hadn't wanted
money but of course he had been admitted to that
nursing home penniless; she had given him money for
tipping and taxis or whatever he needed. He hated
taking her money, he hated that more than anything.

He got off the bus in the City Centre. Other people
were walking about normally, it seemed to him; they
had no problems and big decisions. They looked
vacantly into windows of shops, or screwed their eyes
up against the sunlight to see whether the traffic
lights were green or red. A few early tourists strolled,
everyone else seemed to bustle a bit. He looked at

them wonderingly; most of them would have no problems handling a few glasses of spirits, a few pints, a bottle of wine with their meal, yet a lot of them wouldn't even bother to. He saw with annoyance a couple of Pioneer Pins pass by; that Total Abstinence in order to make reparation to the Sacred Heart always annoyed him deeply. Nine tenths of these fellows didn't know what they were giving up. It was as if he said that he'd give up mangoes or passion fruit, something he'd never tasted. The Lord couldn't be all that pleased with such a sacrifice; the Lord, if he was there at all, must know that these Pioneers were a crowd of hypocritical show-offs. Easy, easy. Stop thinking about drink as some wonderful happiness creator. Don't imagine that a drink suddenly turns the world into an attractive technicolour. The world's fine now, isn't it? He didn't want a drink this moment, did he? No. Well then, what was the problem?

He caught the number ten with agility just as it was about to pull out. There right in front of him was Clare Kelly. 'The lovely Clare . . . well, aren't I steeped?' he said with a mock gallant manner that played to the rest of the bus.

Clare was embarrassed and irritated to have run into him. Gerry could see that. She was a distant, cold sort of woman, he had always thought. Full of sarcasm and the witty answer. Gave poor Des a bloody awful time at home. Des had nothing to say to her these days, he had often told that to Gerry. He had said that he and Clare didn't actually talk, have real conversations; there was always a state of war, where one or the other was winning. Nobody could remember when the war had been declared but it was there, in private as well as in public, putting each other down. Not that there was much in public these days. Clare didn't have much time for her husband's friends. Des preferred it that way. Let her have her meetings and her own life, let her laugh and sneer with her own friends, mock and make little of people. That suited him fine. Gerry had been very sorry for Des, the best of fellows. No matter what things went wrong in his own life at least Emma didn't mock him.

Clare had moved over to make room for him. 'You're looking marvellous,' she said.

'Why wouldn't I, with all it cost?' he said, laughing. 'Can I get your ticket? Two to . . . are you going home or are you off to reform the world somewhere?' He paused as the conductor waited.

'Home,' she laughed at him. 'You haven't changed Gerry, they didn't knock the spirit out of you.'

'No, only the spirits,' he laughed happily, and handed her her ticket like you would give it to a child. 'Here, take this in case we have a fight before we get home and you and I separate.'

'Are you on your way home now from . . . you know?'

'Yes, just released. They gave me back my own clothes, a few quid to keep me going and the names and addresses of people who might take on an ex-con . . .' He laughed, but stopped when he noticed that Clare wasn't laughing at all.

'Wouldn't you think Emma . . . ? It's awful to have you coming out on your own, like this.'

'I wanted to. Emma said she'd come in the car after work, your Des said he'd come for me in a taxi, Brother Jack, the ray of sunshine, said he'd arrive and escort me home after work, Father Vincent said he would come with a pair of wings and a halo and spirit me home . . . but I wanted to come home on my own. You could understand that, couldn't you?'

'Oh yes,' said Clare, managing to get some lofty superiority into the two words.

'Well, how's everything been, out in the real world?'

'Quiet, a bit quieter without you.' She didn't smile as she said it. She said it as though he were a dangerous influence, someone who had been upsetting people. There was ill-concealed regret that he was back in circulation. He smiled at her pleasantly as if he hadn't understood her tone. He had to be very calm, no point in becoming touchy, no seeing insults, fancying slights, imagining hostilities; no running away to hide because people were embarrassed about his treatment; no rushing out to console himself because the world didn't understand. Nice and easy.

'Ah, if that's the case we'll have to liven it up a bit. A quiet world is no use to God, man or the devil, as they say.' He left the subject and drew her attention to some demolition work they could see from the bus. 'Hey, that reminds me,' he said cheerfully, 'did you hear the one about the Irish brickie who came in to this site looking for a job . . .'

Clare Kelly looked at him as he told the story. He looked slimmer and his eyes were clear. He was quite a handsome man in a way. Of course it had been years since she had seen him sober so that made a difference. She wondered, as she had wondered many times, what people saw in him; he had no brain whatsoever. In between his ears he had sawdust.

She smiled politely at the end of the story, but it didn't matter to Gerry because the bus conductor and three people nearby had laughed loudly. And he was really telling the joke to them as much as to Clare.

                    *   *   *

He was pleased to see the flowers. That was very nice
of Emma. He put his little case down in the sitting
room and moved automatically to the cupboard
under the music centre to pour himself a drink. He
had his hand on the door when he remembered. God,
how strong the old habits were. How ridiculous that
in all those weeks in the hospital he never found
himself automatically reaching for some alcohol, but
now here at home . . . . He remembered that nice
young Nurse Dillon saying to him that he would find
it hard to make the normal movements at home
because he would be so accustomed to connecting
them with drink. She had said that some people in-
vented totally new things to do, like drinking Bovril
when they came in to the house. Bovril? He had
wrinkled his nose. Or Marmite, or any unfamiliar
beverage, like hot chocolate. She had been very nice,
that Nurse Dillon, regarded the whole thing as a bit of
bad luck like getting measles; she had even given him
a small Bovril last night and said that he might laugh
but it could well come in handy. He had said that he
was such a strong character he would go to the drinks
cupboard and pour the bottles down the sink. Nurse
Dillon said that he might find his wife had already
done that for him.

    Gerry opened the doors. Inside there were six large
bottles of red lemonade, six of slimline tonic, six of
Coca Cola. There was a bottle of Lime Cordial and a
dozen cans of tomato juice. He blinked at them. It
was a little high-handed of Emma to have poured
away all his alcohol without so much as a by-your-
leave. He felt a flush of annoyance creep up his neck.
In fact it was bloody high-handed of her. What did all

this business about trusting him, and relying on him, and not pressurising him, mean if she had poured his drink away? There had been the remains of a case of wine, and two bottles of whiskey there. Money to buy things didn't grow on trees.

Very, very upset he went out to the kitchen and put his hands on the sink deliberately to relax himself. He looked at the plug hole. Without a word of consultation she had poured about twenty pounds worth of drink down there. Then his eye fell on a box in the corner of the kitchen, with a piece of writing paper sellotaped to it. 'Gerry. I took these out of the sitting room cupboard to make room for the other lot. Tell me where you want them put. E.' His eyes filled with tears. He wiped his face with the back of his hand and sniffed as he struck the match to light the gas to boil the kettle to make his cup of Bovril.

*   *   *

Mrs Moore had rung once or twice during the day, but there had been no reply. That Emma and her precious job. What was she except a glorified typist? Just because she was in Montrose, just because she had sat at the same table as Gay Byrne in the coffee shop, and walked down a corridor with Mike Murphy, just because she had given Valerie McGovern a lift and had a long chat with Jim O'Neill from Radio Two, did that make her special? Oh no, it didn't, just a clerk is all she was. And a clerk with a heart of stone. The girl had no feeling in her. Wouldn't any normal person have taken the day off to welcome her husband back from six weeks in hospital? But not Emma. The poor lad had to come back to an empty house.

'Ah, there you are, Gerry, how are you, are you feeling all right now, did you have a good rest?'

'Like a fighting cock, mother, grand, grand altogether.'

'And did they give you medicines, injections, did they look after you properly? I can't think why you didn't go to Vincent's. Isn't it beside you? And you have the Voluntary Health.'

'Oh, I know, mother, but they don't have the course there. I had the whole course, you know, and thank God it seems to have worked. But of course, you never know. You're never really sure.'

'What do you mean you're not sure, you're all right! Didn't they have you in there for six weeks? Gerry? Do you hear me? If you don't feel all right, you should see someone else. Someone we know.'

'No, Mother, I'm fine, really fine.'

'So what did they tell you to do, rest more?'

'No, the contrary in fact, keep busy, keep active, tire myself out even.'

'But wasn't that what had you in there, because you were tired out?'

'Don't you know as well as I do what had me in there? It was the drink.'

His mother was silent.

'But it's all right now, I know what I was doing to myself and it's all over.'

'A lot of nonsense they talk. Don't let them get you involved in their courses, Gerry. You're fine, there's nothing the matter with you, you can have a drink as well as the next man.'

'You're not helping me, mother, I know you mean well but those are not the facts.'

'Facts, facts . . . don't bother with *your* facts, with *their* facts up in that place. The fact is that your

Father drank as much as he liked every evening of his life and he lived to be seventy, Lord have mercy on him. He would have lived to be far more if he hadn't had that stroke.'

'I know, Mother, I know, and you're very good to be so concerned, but, believe me, I know best. I've been listening to them for six weeks. I can't touch drink any more. It's labelled poison as far as I'm concerned. It's sad, but there it is.'

'Oh, we'll see, we'll see. A lot of modern rubbish. Emma was explaining it to me. A lot of nonsense. People had more to do with their time when I was young than to be reading and writing these pamphlets about not eating butter and not smoking and not drinking. Wasn't life fine in the old days before all these new worries came to plague us, tell me, wasn't it?'

'It was, Mother, it was,' said Gerry wearily.

*　　　*　　　*

It *had* been fine for a while. When Gerry and Emma got married he had a good career. There was a lot of money to be made from advertising in the sixties: one day it had been a bottle and an elegant glass, another it had been a consultation about photographing new banks, the sites, and personnel, the buildings. He had known all the agencies, there was no shortage of work. Emma had been so enthusiastic about his work — she had said it was much more vibrant and alive than her own. She had taught book-keeping and accountancy for beginners in a technical school. She never called it a career; she had been delighted to leave it when Paul was expected, and she had never seemed to want to go back when Helen was off to school and out of the way, and that was a good seven years ago. Now that the bottom had fallen out of the market in advertising and there were no good photographic jobs left, Emma wasn't able to get back into teaching either. They didn't want people who had opted out for fifteen years, why should they? That's why she was up in the television station doing typing, and thinking herself lucky to get the job.

They had said in the nursing home it wasn't very helpful to look back too much on the past; it made you feel sorry for yourself, or wistful. Or else you began to realise what had happened was inevitable, and that wasn't a good idea either. You started to think you had no responsibility for your actions. So let's not think of the past, the old days when life was fine. He made the Bovril and took it, sniffing it suspiciously, into the sitting room. Hard not to think of the old days. A picture of their wedding in the silver frame, laughing and slim, both of them. His own father and both Emma's parents, now dead, smiled out more formally. His mother had looked confident, as if she knew she would be a long liver.

Then the pictures of Paul and Helen, the series he had done; they looked magnificent, people said, on an alcove wall, a record of the seventies children growing up, turning into people before your eyes. But they had stopped turning into people photographically about five years ago. The children seemed stuck in a time warp of his making.

He looked back at the wedding picture and again he felt the prickling in his nose and eyes that he had felt when he read Emma's note in the kitchen. Poor girl, she was only a girl, she was only thirty-nine years old and she had been keeping four people for two years on a typist's salary. That's really what it boiled down to. Of course, there had been the odd cheque coming in for him, the royalties from some of those coffee table books; a little here for a print he'd taken from stock for someone's calendar, a little there for a permission to reprint. But he had cashed those cheques and spent them himself. Emma had kept the family. God, he would make it up to her, he really would. He would make up every penny and every hour of worry and anxiety. He wiped his eyes again, he must be big and strong. Gerry Moore was home again, he was going to take over his family once more.

*   *   *

Emma hadn't liked to make a phone call while the office was quiet. It was too important a call, she couldn't suddenly hang up if she felt that people were listening to her. Anxiously she watched the clock, knowing that he must be home by now, wishing that she had done more to make the place welcoming, mentally ticking off the shopping she had done at lunchtime; she was going to make them a celebratory meal. She hoped he wasn't regretting his decision to come home alone; going back to an empty house, to a changed lifestyle after six weeks in a hospital, it wasn't such a good idea. To her great delight the office filled up with people and she was able to turn her back and call home.

'Hallo?' His voice sounded a little tentative and even snuffly, as if he had a cold.

'You're very welcome home, love,' she said.

'You're great, Emma,' he said.

'No I'm not, but I'll be home in an hour and a half and I can't wait to see you. It's grand you're back.'

'The place is great. Thank you for the flowers and

the card.'

'Wait till you see what we're going to have tonight — you'll think you're in a first class hotel.'

'I'm cured, you know that.'

'Of course I do. You're very strong and you've got a terrific life ahead of you, we all have.'

His voice definitely sounded as if he had a cold, but maybe he was crying — she wouldn't mention it in case it was crying and it upset him that she noticed.

'The kids will be in any minute, you'll have plenty of company.'

'I'm fine, I'm fine. You're very good to ring. I thought you couldn't make calls there.' She had told him that the organisation expressly forbade private calls in or out. She had said this to stop him ringing when he was drunk.

'Oh, I sneaked one because today is special,' she said.

'I'll soon have you out of that place, never fear,' he said.

She remembered suddenly how much he hated her being the breadwinner.

'That's great,' she said. 'See you very soon.' She hung up. He sounded grand. Please, please God may it be all right. There was a man in RTE who hadn't touched a drop in twenty years, he told her. A lovely man, great fun, very successful, and yet he said he was a desperate tearaway when he was a young fellow. Maybe Gerry would be like him. She must believe. She must have faith in him. Otherwise the cure wouldn't work.

*   *   *

Paul came home first. He shuffled a bit when he saw his father sitting reading the *Evening Press* in the big armchair. It wasn't just six weeks since he had seen such a scene, it was much longer; Dad hadn't been round much for ages.

He put down his books on the table.

'You're back, isn't that great?' he said.

Gerry stood up and went and put both hands on his son's shoulders. 'Paul, will you forgive me?' he asked, looking straight into the boy's eyes.

Paul squirmed, and flushed. He had never been so embarrassed. What was Dad saying these awful corny lines for? It was worse than some awful old film on the television. Would he forgive him? It was yucky.

'Sure, Dad,' he said, wriggling away from the hands. 'Did you get the bus home?'

'No, seriously, I have been very anxious to say this to you for a few weeks, and I'm glad to have a chance before there's anyone else here.'

'Dad, it doesn't matter. Aren't you fine now, isn't that all that counts?'

'No, of course it isn't. There's no point in having a son unless you can talk to him. I just want to say that for too long this house hasn't been my responsibility. I was like someone who ran away, but I'm back, and it will all be like it was when you were a baby and don't remember . . . but this time you're grown up.'

'Yes,' said Paul, bewildered.

'And if I make rules and regulations about homework and helping in the house, I'm not going to expect you to take them meekly. You can say to me, what kind of sod are you to be ordering us about, where were you when I needed you? I'll listen to you, Paul, and I'll answer. Together we'll make this a proper family.'

'I wouldn't say things like that. I'm glad you're home, Dad, and that it's cured, the illness bit, honestly.'

'Good boy.' His father took out a handkerchief and blew his nose. 'You're a very good boy. Thank you.'

Paul's heart sank. Poor old Dad wasn't in good shape at all, maybe his mind had gone in that place, talking all this sentimental crap, and tears in his eyes. Oh shit, now he couldn't ask to go over to Andy's house. It would cause a major upheaval and maybe his father would burst into tears. God, wasn't it depressing.

*　　　*　　　*

Helen went into the presbytery on her way home in order to speak to Father Vincent.

'Is anything wrong?' The priest immediately assumed the worst.

'No, Mummy keeps saying there's no crisis, so it must all be fine, but I came to ask if you'd call in tonight on some excuse. If you could make up some reason why you had to call . . .'

'No, child, your father's coming home tonight, I don't want to intrude on the family, you'll all want to be together. Not tonight, I'll call in again sometime, maybe in a day or two.'

'I think it would be better if you came in now, at the beginning, honestly.'

The priest was anxious to do the best thing but didn't know what it was. 'Tell me, Helen, what would I say, what would I do? Why would I be a help? If you could explain that to me then I would, of course.'

Helen was thoughtful for a moment. 'It's hard to say, Father Vincent, but I'm thinking of other times. Things were never so bad when you were there, they used to put on a bit of manners in front of you, you know, Mummy and Daddy, they wouldn't be fighting and saying awful things to each other.'

'Yes, but I don't think . . .'

'It mightn't have looked great to you, but if you weren't there, Daddy would be drinking much more and saying awful things and Mummy would be shouting at him not to upset us . . .'

The child looked very upset; Father Vincent spoke quickly. 'I know, I know, and a lot of homes that sort of thing happens in. Don't think yours is the only one where a voice is raised, let me assure you. But you're forgetting one thing, Helen, your father is cured. Thank God he took this cure himself. It was very hard and the hardest bit was having to admit that he couldn't handle drink. He now has admitted this and he's fine, he's really fine. I've been to see him, you know, up in the home. I know he didn't want you children going there, but he's a new man, in fact he's the old man, his old self, and there won't be a thing to worry about.'

'But he's still Daddy.'

'Yes, but he's Daddy without drink. He's in grand form, you'll be delighted with him. No, I won't come in tonight, Helen, but I'll give a ring over the week end and maybe call round for a few minutes.'

Helen looked mutinous. 'I thought priests were meant to help the community. That's what you always say when you come up to the school to talk to us.'

'I am helping, by not poking my nose in. Believe me, I'm older than you are.'

'That's the thing people say when they've no other argument,' Helen said.

* * *

Emma cycled down the road and saw Helen moodily kicking a stone.

'Are you only coming home now?' she asked, annoyed that Helen hadn't been back to welcome Gerry earlier.

'I called in to see Father Vincent on the way,' said Helen.

'What about?' Emma was alarmed.

'Private business, you're not to ask people what goes on between them and their confessor, it's the secrecy of the confessional.'

'Sorry,' said Emma. 'He's not coming round here tonight by any awful chance, is he?'

Helen looked at her mother with a puzzled look. 'No, he's not actually.'

'Good, I want us to be on our own today. You run ahead and say hello to your father, I'll be in in a moment.'

Unwillingly Helen walked on: as she turned in the gate she saw her mother take out a comb and mirror and pat her hair. How silly Mummy could be at times. What was she combing her hair for now? There was nobody at home to see her. You'd think she'd have combed it when she was in RTE where she might meet people who'd be looking at her.

* * *

Gerry gave Helen a hug that nearly squeezed the breath out of her.

'You're very grown up, you know, a real teenager,' he said.

'Oh Dad, it isn't that long since you've seen me, it's only a few weeks. You sound like an old sailor coming back from months abroad.'

'That's what I feel like, that's exactly the way I feel — how clever of you to spot it,' he said.

Helen and Paul exchanged fairly alarmed glances. Then they heard Mum's bicycle clanking against the garage wall and everyone looked at the back door. She burst in through the scullery and into the kitchen. She looked flushed from riding the bicycle; she had a huge bag of groceries which she had taken from the basket. In her jeans and shirt she looked very young, Gerry thought.

They hugged each other in the kitchen, rocking backwards and forwards as if the children were not there, as if Gerry wasn't holding a second mug of Bovril in his hand and as if Emma weren't holding the shopping in hers.

'Thank God, thank God,' Gerry kept saying.

'You're back, you're back again,' Emma said over and over.

Solemn-eyed, their children looked at them from the door into the hall. Their faces seemed to say that this was almost as bad as what they had been through before.

*   *   *

The telephone rang as they were having supper. Emma, her mouth full of prawns, said she'd get it.

'It's probably your mother, she said she'd ring.'

'She has,' said Gerry.

It was Jack. He had been kept late at the shop. Mr

Power had decided at the last moment that all the furniture in the show-rooms should be shifted around so that the cleaners could get at the place from a different angle. Emma spent two and a half minutes listening to a diatribe against Mr Power; she grunted and murmured soothingly. Then the tone of Jack's voice changed, it became conspiratorial.

'Is he home?' he whispered.

'Yes, thank God, he came home this afternoon. Looks as fit as a fiddle. We'll all have to go up there and be pampered, I tell you.' She laughed and sounded light-hearted, hoping Jack would catch her mood.

'And is there . . . is there any sign of . . .?'

'Oh yes, very cheerful, and he sends you his good wishes — we're just having a welcome home supper for him actually.' Would Jack take this heavy hint, was there the remotest chance that he might realise he had rung at a meal-time?

'Is he listening to you, there in the room?'

'Yes, that's right.'

'Well, I obviously can't talk now. I'll ring later, when he's asleep maybe.'

'Why don't you ring in the morning, Jack, say, late morning. Saturday's a good day, we'll all be around then, and you could have a word with Gerry himself. Right?'

'I'm not sure if I'll be able to ring in the late morning.'

'Well, sometime tomorrow . . .' She looked back at Gerry and affectionately they both raised their eyes to the ceiling. 'If only you'd get a phone, we could ring you. I hate you having to find the coins always for calls.'

'There's no point in paying the rental for a telephone, and they charge you any figure that comes into their heads, I tell you, for the number of calls. No, I'm better to use the coin box, it's not far away. It's just that there's often a lot of kids around on a Saturday.'

'Well, whenever you can, Jack.'

'You're marvellous with him, marvellous. Not many women would be able to cope like you.'

'That's right,' she laughed. He was such a lonely figure she didn't like to choke him off too quickly. 'And how are you keeping yourself?' she asked.

Jack told her at length: he told her that he had a bad neck which resulted from a draught that came through a door which Mr Power insisted on being open. He told her that people weren't buying as much furniture as they used to, and that this craze for going to auctions and stripping things down was ruining the trade. She motioned to Paul, who was nearest to her, to pass her plate. She was annoyed with Jack's timing and his insensitivity, but if she hung up she would feel guilty and she wanted to be able to relax tonight of all nights without another problem crowding her mind.

She looked over at the table as she let Jack ramble on; they all seemed to be getting on all right. Gerry looked great, he had lost weight too. The two of them were much more like their wedding photograph than they had ever been. His jaw was leaner, his eyes were bright, he was being endlessly patient with the kids, too, which was a lot more difficult than it sounded. Helen in particular was as prickly as a hedgehog, and Paul was restless. Jack seemed to be coming to an end. He would ring tomorrow and talk to Gerry, he hoped Gerry appreciated all that she did for him, going out and earning a living, keeping the family together. If only he had had sense long ago

and not put so much at risk. 'But it's all fine now,'
Emma said wearily. Jack agreed doubtfully and hung
up.

'Was he repenting of my wicked life?' asked Gerry.

'A bit,' Emma laughed. Gerry laughed, and after a
moment the children laughed too. It was the nearest
to normal living they had known for about four
years.

*   *   *

Gerry spent Saturday in his study. It was a four-bed-
roomed house and when they had bought it they had
decided at once that the master bedroom should
be his study. Other men rented offices, so it made
sense that the big bedroom with the good light should
be where Gerry worked. The little bathroom attached
to the bedroom was turned into a darkroom. Once it
had been a miracle of organisation: a huge old-fashioned chest of drawers, a lovely piece of furniture
holding all his up-to-date filing system. As efficient as
any steel filing cabinet, only a hundred times more
attractive. The lighting was good, the walls were hung
with pictures; some of a single object, like his famous
picture of a diamond; some were pictures that told a
success story. Gerry receiving an award here, Gerry
sharing a joke there. Then there was the huge, bulging
desk, full recently of bills or handouts, or refusals or
rubbish, making a mockery of the filing.

He had sighed when he saw it, but Emma had been
beside him.

'Tell me what you want except a couple of black
plastic sacks to get rid of the rubbish,' she had said.

'And a bottle of Paddy to get rid of the pain of
looking at it,' he had said.

185

'You poor old divil, it's not that bad is it?' she said lightly.

'No,' he said, 'I'm only being dramatic. I'll need a dozen plastic bags.'

'Don't throw everything out,' she said, alarmed.

'I'll throw a lot out, love, I have to start again from scratch, you know that.'

'You did it once, you'll do it again,' she said and went downstairs.

*   *   *

Gerry made himself four big, sweeping categories: Real Rubbish; Browsing Through later Rubbish; For the Filing Cabinet, and Contacts for the New Life.

Almost everything seemed to fit into those; he was pleased with himself and even hummed as the marathon sorting work went on.

Emma heard him as she made the beds and she paused and remembered. Remembered what it used to be like, a cheerful confident Gerry, whistling and humming in his study, then running lightly down the stairs and into his car off to another job. In those days there was a big pad beside the phone where she put down the time the person called, their name, their business. She had always sounded so efficient and helpful; clients had often asked was she Mr Moore's partner and she would laugh and say a very permanent partner — they had found that entertaining. For months, years, the phone had hardly rung for Gerry, except a call from Des Kelly or a complaint from his brother Jack, or a list of complaints about something from his mother. Should she dare to believe that things were ever going to be normal again? Was it tempting fate to believe that he might really stay off the drink and build his business up? She didn't know. She had nobody to ask, really. She couldn't go to Al Anon and discuss it with other wives and families, because that somehow wasn't fair. It would be different if Gerry had joined Alcoholics Anonymous; then she would be able to join something that went hand in hand with it, but no. Gerry didn't want to go to some room every week and hear a lot of bores standing up and saying, 'I'm Tadgh, I'm an alcoholic.' No, the course was the modern way of dealing with things and he had done that and been cured.

She sighed; why was she blaming him? He had done it his way and he had done it. For six weeks in that home he had become stronger and more determined. For two days now at home he was managing. She must stop fearing and suspecting and dreading, dreading things like the first phone call from Des Kelly, the first row, the first disappointment. Would he have the strength to go on being sunny after all these?

*　　　*　　　*

Gerry had tucked three bags of Real Rubbish into the garage, all neatly tied at the neck. He insisted that Emma come up and admire what he had done. The room still looked very much of a shambles to her, but he seemed to see some order in it, so she enthused. He had found three cheques as well — out of date, but they could be re-dated. They totalled over £200.00. He was very pleased with himself for finding them and said that it called for a dinner out.

'Are you sure they weren't re-issued already? One's three years old.' Emma wished she hadn't said it. It sounded grudging. She spoke on quickly. 'If they have been, so what? You're quite right, where will we go?'

He suggested a restaurant which was also a pub. She kept the smile on her face unchanged. There was going to be a lot of this kind of thing, she'd better learn to get used to it. Just because Gerry Moore had to cut alcohol out of his life, it seemed a vain hope that the rest of Ireland would decide to stop selling it, serving it and advertising it.

'I'd love that,' she said enthusiastically. 'I'll wash my hair in honour of it.'

Des Kelly rang a bit later.

'How are you, old son?' he asked.

'Ready for the Olympics,' Gerry said proudly.

'Do they include a few jars of orange juice, or is that more than flesh and blood could stand?'

'Oh, this flesh and blood can stand anything, but not tonight — I'm taking Emma out to a slap-up meal to say thank you.'

'Thank you?'

'For holding the fort and all while I was above in the place.'

'Oh yes, of course, of course . . .'

'But tomorrow, Des, as usual. Twelve thirty?'

'Great stuff. Are you sure you won't . . .'

'I'm sure, I'm sure. Tell me about yourself — what have you been doing?'

Des told him about a script which he had sweated blood on which was refused by a jumped-up person who knew nothing, and he told him about one that had gone well and got a few nice write-ups in the paper.

'Oh yeah, I remember that, that was before I went in,' Gerry said.

'Was it? Maybe it was. The time gets confused. Well, what else? The same as usual. I've missed you, old son, I really have. There's not much of a laugh around. I tried leaving Madigan's and I went to McCloskey's and I went down to the Baggot Street area for a bit, Waterloo House, Searson's, Mooney's, but there was no one to talk to. I'm glad you're out.'

'So am I.'

'Were they desperate to you in there?'

'Not at all, they were fine, it was up to me. If I didn't want to go along with any of it I didn't have to.'

'Well, that's good.'

'And you can relax, I'm not going to be producing leaflets at you and telling you that you should cut it down a bit.' Gerry laughed as he said it. Des laughed too, with some relief.

'Thanks be to God. See you tomorrow, old son, and enjoy the second honeymoon night out.'

Gerry wished that he had found cheques for two thousand, not two hundred, then he would have taken Emma on a second honeymoon. Maybe when he got himself set up again he'd be able to do that. He'd think about it. It would be great to be out with a villa hired for two weeks in one of these places like Lanzarotte. There was a fellow in the nursing home who had bought a house there with a whole group of other Irish people, like a little complex of them out there. They made their own fun, they brought out a ton of duty-free — well, forget that side of it, but there were marvellous beaches and great weather even in winter. He went back to his sorting. It was the section on contacts that was giving him most trouble. A lot of agencies seemed to have changed, merged with others or gone out of business. A lot of new names. A lot of bad blood with some of the old names — work promised and not done, work done but not accepted. Jesus, it might be easier starting afresh in another country. Australia? This place was a village, what one knew at lunchtime everyone else knew at tea time. Still, nobody had said it was going to be easy.

*   *   *

Gerry was in very low form by the time it came to dress up for going out. The children were out of the house: Paul was with Andy as usual and Helen had gone to a tennis lesson. She had asked that morning at breakfast if the household budget would cover tennis lessons. She didn't really mind if it didn't, and she wasn't going to be a strain on people, but if the money was there she would like to join the group. Gerry had insisted she join, and said that he would get her a new racquet if she showed any promise. She had departed in high spirits and would stay and have tea with one of her friends who lived near the courts.

Emma was fixing her newly washed hair; she sat in a slip at the dressing table and watched Gerry come in. At first she had thought he might want them to go to bed. They hadn't made love last night, just lay side by side holding hands until he drifted off to sleep. This seemed like a good time. But no, that was the last thing on his mind so she was glad he hadn't really attended to her slightly flirtatious remarks. It didn't seem so much of a rejection if he hadn't heard what she had said. His brow looked dark.

'It will be nice to go out, I'm really looking forward to it.'

'Don't rub it in. I *know* you haven't been out for a

long time,' he said.

She bit back the aggrieved retort. 'What will you have, do you think?' she said, searching desperately for some uncontroversial side to it all.

'How the hell do I know until I see the menu? I don't have radar eyes. I'm not inspired by the Holy Ghost to know what's going to be served.'

She laughed. She felt like throwing the brush and every single thing on the dressing table at him. She felt like telling him what to do with his dinner invitation — an invitation she would have to pay for anyway until those out-of-date cheques were cleared — if they ever were. She felt like saying the house had been a peaceful and better place while he was in the nursing home. But she managed to say, 'I know. Deep down I'm just a glutton, I expect. Don't mind me.'

He was shaving at the small handbasin in their bedroom. His eyes caught hers and he smiled. 'You're too good for me.'

'No I'm not, I'm what you deserve,' she said lightly.

In the car he took her hand.

'Sorry,' he said.

'Don't mind about it,' she said.

'The night just seemed hard ahead of us, no wine with the dinner and all.'

'I know,' she said sympathetically.

'But you're to have wine, you must, otherwise the whole thing's a nonsense.'

'You know I don't mind one way or the other. You know I can easily have a Perrier water.'

'Part of the fact of being cured is not to mind other people. It was just that I got a bit low there, inside, in the house, I don't know. I'm fine now.'

'Of course you are, and I'll certainly have a glass or

two if it doesn't annoy you.' She put the key into the ignition and drove off.

Technically he was allowed to drive again now, but he hadn't reapplied, or whatever you were meant to do. And in the last few months he wouldn't have been able to drive. She had offered him the keys as they came to the car and he had shaken his head.

In the bar, as they looked at their menus, they met a couple they hadn't seen for a while. Emma saw the wife nudge her husband and point over at them. After what looked a careful scrutiny he came over.

'Gerry Moore, I haven't seen you looking so respectable for years. And Emma . . .' They greeted him with little jokes and little laughs; both of them patted their flatter stomachs while the man said they must have been at a health farm, they looked so well. Emma said she owed hers to her bicycle and Gerry said that, alas, he owed his to laying off the booze. It was like the first hurdle in an obstacle race. Emma knew from the whispers between the couple that there would be many more. The news would get around, people would come to inspect, to see if it was true. Gerry Moore, that poor old soak, back to his former self, you never saw anything like it, doesn't touch a drop now, made a fortune last year, back on top as a photographer, you never saw anything like him and the wife. Please. Please, God. Please let it happen.

*　　*　　*

Father Vincent called around on Saturday night and knocked for a long time at the door. The car was gone, Emma's bicycle was there, and there was no reply. He assumed they must all be out at some family gathering. But that child had seemed so white and worried, he hoped that Gerry hadn't broken out immediately and been taken back into the home. He debated with himself for a long time about whether to leave a note or not. In the end he decided against it. Suppose poor Gerry had broken out and been taken back in, it would be a sick sort of thing to leave a welcome home card. Father Vincent wished, as he often did, that he had second sight.

Paul came home from Andy's and turned on the television. Helen came in shortly afterwards; they sat with peanut butter sandwiches and glasses of milk and watched happily. They heard voices, and a key turn in the lock.

'Oh Lord,' said Paul, 'I'd forgotten *he* was back, pick up the glass, Helen, give me those plates. We're meant to be running a tidy ship here!' Helen laughed at the imitation of her father's voice, but she looked out into the hall anxiously to make sure that Daddy wasn't drunk.

*　　*　　*

It was very expensive having Gerry home. Emma realised this, but couldn't quite think why. She realised that he wasn't spending any money on drink; apart from that one Saturday night out they didn't entertain people. Gerry bought no clothes or household things. Why then was her money not stretching as far as it used to? A lot of it might be on stationery and stamps. Gerry was as good as his word about writing to people with ideas — just bright, cheery letters which said, without having to spell it out, I'm back, I'm cured and I'm still a great photographer. Then he liked to cook new things, things that he wouldn't associate with alcohol. Together they had spent a great deal of money on curry ingredients, but then he had tired of it, and said it wasn't worth all the trouble — they could slip out and buy a good curry if they needed one. She didn't grudge it, but she had been so used to accounting for every penny carefully, putting this little bit there towards the electricity, this towards the gas, and that towards the phone. She didn't know what she was going to do when the next bills came in. And talking of bills, what the phone bill was going to be like made her feel weak around the legs.

Gerry had been talking to somebody in Limerick for nearly fifteen minutes one night, and he mentioned calls to Manchester and London. She had said nothing; she just prayed that the rewards and results of all these phone calls might be felt by the time the telephone bill came in.

*   *   *

Gerry's mother thought that he wasn't himself at all since he came out of that place. He had gone up to see her and the visit was not a success. She had bought a naggin of whiskey for him specially. It was in the glass-fronted cupboard there beside the china dogs. Ah, go on, surely one wouldn't do him any harm.

'No, Mother. That's the whole point. I've got something wrong with my insides, it turns to poison in me. I told you this. Emma explained . . .'

'Huh, Emma. High-brow talk. Allergy addiction. I'm sick of it.'

'Yes, Mother, so am I,' Gerry's patience was ebbing, 'but it happens to be true.'

'Look, have just the one and we'll quit fighting,' his mother had said.

'It would be easy for me to say Thank You Mother, to hold it here in my fist and when you weren't looking to throw it away. But I can't do that. I can't bloody do it. Can you have the wit of a half-wit and understand that?'

'There's no need to shout at me, I've quite enough to put up with,' his Mother had said, and then she had started to cry.

'Listen, Mother, give me the bottle you so kindly bought for me. I'll give it to Father Vincent for his sale of work, he can use it on the tombola or something. Then it won't be wasted.'

'I will not. If I bought whiskey it will be there to offer to someone who has the manners to take it.'

No other subject managed to bring them on to the same plane. Gerry left, and hoped that nobody who lived on earth had such a poor relationship with a parent as he had. That was the day that he went home and found Paul fighting with Emma in the kitchen. They hadn't heard him come in.

'But *WHY*, if you could tell me *WHY* I might do it. He's not an invalid, he's not soft in the head, so why does he want to play happy families sitting down to supper together every night? If I go over to Andy's after supper it's too late, then the evening's spoiled.'

'Ask Andy here.'

'No fear.'

Gerry came in and looked at them, first one and then another.

'Please spend the evening with your friend tonight, Paul. Emma, can I have a word with you in my study when you're ready?'

He walked on upstairs. He heard Helen, giggling

nervously.

'That's just the voice that Reverend Mother uses when she's going to expel someone,' she said, stifling her laughs.

* * *

'The boy is right. I am not soft in the head. I get weary of all these family meals, if you must know.'

'I thought with my being out all day and you getting back into a routine . . .'

'You thought, you thought, you thought . . . what else is it in this house except what you think?'

She looked at him in disbelief.

'I mean it, Emma, morning, noon and night . . .'

Two large tears fell down her face and two more were on the way down like raindrops on a window. She didn't even brush them aside; she didn't try to deny it, to reason with him, or to agree with him. She just looked beaten.

'Well, say something, Emma, if you don't agree with me say something.'

'What is there to say?' she sobbed. 'I love you so much and everything I do seems to hurt you, God Almighty, how can I do what will please you? I'm obviously doing all the wrong things.'

He put his arms around her and stroked her hair. 'Stop, stop,' he said. She cried into his chest.

'You're very good. I'm really a shit, a terrible shit.' She made a muffled denial into his shirt.

'And I love you too and need you . . .'

She looked up at him with a tear-stained face. 'Do you?'

'Of course,' he said.

Downstairs, Helen said, 'They've gone into the bedroom, isn't that odd?'

Paul said, 'He can't be going to expel her then.'

Helen said, 'What do you think they're doing?'

Paul laughed knowingly, 'I'll give you one guess,' he said.

Helen was horrified. 'They can't be. They're much too old.'

Paul said, 'Why else have they closed the door?'

'God, that's awful, that's all we need.'

Father Vincent called just then. Helen was so embarrassed when she recognised his shape through the door that she ran back for Paul.

'I can't tell him what we think,' she said. 'You couldn't tell a priest something like that.'

Paul let him in. 'Mum and Dad are upstairs at the moment, having a bit of a lie down. If you don't mind, Father, I won't disturb them.'

'Of course, of course,' Father Vincent looked confused. 'But can I get you a cup of tea, coffee?' The priest said he didn't want to be any trouble.

'A drink?'

'No, no, heavens, no.'

'We have drink. Dad insists it be kept there for visitors.'

Father Vincent stayed for about ten minutes with no drink and hardly any conversation. When he was at the porch again, he looked timidly at the stairs. 'If your father has taken a turn for the worse and your Mother wants any help, she only has to call on me.' Paul said that he didn't think Mother wanted any help just now, and when the door was safely closed he and Helen rolled around the sitting room floor laughing at the idea of leading Father Vincent upstairs, knocking on the bedroom door and calling out that Father Vincent wanted to know if Mother wanted any help or could manage on her own.

Gerry and Emma lay in their big bed and Gerry said, 'It's been so long, I was afraid to, I was afraid, in case . . .' Emma said, 'You were lovely as you were always lovely.' She lay counting the days since her last period; she was safe, she had to be safe. The very notion of becoming pregnant, now, was too much to contemplate. She had stopped taking the pill two years ago. It was said to have some side effects and women were warned not to stay on it for ever. And what on earth had been the point of taking the pill when there was simply no risk of becoming pregnant?

*   *   *

Jack was sorry that Gerry was back. It sort of put a stop to his Monday visits. He used to visit Gerry on a Sunday and then took the bus to their house on a Monday night after work to report on what he saw, what he said, what was said back to him and what he thought. The first couple of times they had been eager to know what he reported because they still hadn't got used to life without Gerry. Then, after that, it had become a little ritual. Emma used to cook a nice meal, and then they would all wash up. Jack would sit down in the comfort of a nice big sitting room, not his own cramped little bed-sitter. They used to watch television, while Emma sometimes did mending; the television set was turned low so as not to disturb the two children who did homework. All through April and May Jack had been involved in their life. There was no excuse for him to come any more.

He had liked those evenings sitting there with Emma; she had been so nice and interested in everything he had been doing at work. It was so cosy.

Gerry must have been a madman, stark staring mad to throw away all his money and his good living and spend time drinking with a crowd of eejits. You wouldn't mind a man who had nothing at home, but a man who had Emma. It was past understanding.

*　　　*　　　*

It seemed a very long summer for everyone. Father Vincent spent a lot of time wondering what he had done to offend the Moores; every time he went there those two young children, who had seemed nice and normal at one stage, were exceedingly silly with giggles. Gerry wanted to hear no inspiring tales of how others triumphed, he had said curtly, and Emma was too busy to say more than the time of day. She had taken some home typing and had rung him once to enquire whether there was any parish work to be done on a professional basis. He had said they would always be glad of some voluntary help, but she had said sorry, that she was not yet in a position to be able to offer that.

Mrs Moore thought that Gerry had become short-tempered and intolerant. Her grandchildren never came near her, and that Emma seemed to be too busy even to talk to her on the telephone.

Paul fell in love with Andy's sister, but Andy's whole family, sister and all, went to Greece for a month. If Paul had two hundred pounds he could have gone out to visit them. His Dad had said he could bloody earn it if he wanted it, and his Mum had said he must be a selfish little rat to think that money like that was available for a holiday for him.

Helen was very bored and very worried. She had become very ugly suddenly, she thought, after years

of looking quite reasonable; now, when it was important, she had become revolting-looking. In books
people's mothers helped them when this kind of thing
happened, lent them make-up and bought them dresses. In real life her Mum told her to stop snivelling,
there would be time enough for that later.

Des felt the summer was long too. He had nothing
but admiration for Gerry — he sat there with the best
of them, bought his round like any man, but it wasn't
the same. Des could never relax like he had, he
couldn't get it out of his head that he was waiting for
Gerry to start, to catch up on the rest of them. It was
restless drinking with him. God damn it, Gerry was
very extreme; when he was going on that batter he
was a fierce drinker, got them barred from several
places, but now that he'd had a fright, instead of
taking it nice and easy like any normal person and
just watching it, here he was like a bloody Pioneer,
sitting there with a glass of lime and soda or whatever he drank nowadays.

Gerry found the summer slow. He found the
replies to his letters even slower, and the offers of any
work were the slowest of all. How could the whole
photography world have collapsed without his
noticing it? There must be people getting work; he
saw their pictures in the advertisements, on the television, in the magazines. 'Maybe,' Emma had said,
'maybe you should show them what you can do *now*,
rather than old portfolios, maybe you should get a
collection for another book together?' But did Emma
have a clue of any sort how long it took to put a
book together? You didn't go out with a camera and
snap 150 things and mark them pages one to one hundred and fifty. There was a theme, there was an interest, there was a commission: a lot of the pictures

had been done and paid for already in somebody else's time. Oh, it was all so slow getting back, and it had seemed so very fast, the fall down the ladder. Or was he just being melodramatic?

Emma realised one day during that endless summer that she had no friend. Not no friends but not even one friend. There was nobody she could talk to about Gerry. There never had been. Her mother had thought he was a little too flash for her and her father had wondered about security. But no matter who had asked her to marry them her mother would have seen flashness and her father suspected insecurity all around him. She never talked to her sister about anything except her sister's five children, all of whom seemed to be doing spectacularly well in exams at any given season of the year. She couldn't talk to her mother-in-law, she certainly couldn't talk to that Des Kelly, who always looked at her as if she were a particularly dangerous kind of snake. Poor Jack was so kind and anxious to help, but really the man was so limited, he couldn't have a serious conversation about Gerry's future to save his life. She had formed an unreasonable dislike of Father Vincent who used to be quite a friend of theirs ten years ago. He had always been quick with liberal attitudes and a broad spectrum but that was not what she needed now. She needed specific advice. It was now four months since Gerry had come home from that nursing home; he had not earned one penny from his trade of photography. To complain about that seemed untimely and ungracious because after all, the man had not touched one drop of alcohol either. There was no point in going to the nursing home and asking the doctors. They had asked her to be co-operative and not to boss him around. She thought that she was doing that part of it. But Lord God, how long would it go on? Already the small debts were building up — paradoxically more frightening than when he had been drinking and the bill from the off-license would arrive. Those drink bills had a terrifying unreality about them. Today's bills, high telephone charges, photography equipment, printing costs, expensive cuts of meat, they had a ring of permanency. And what Emma wanted to know was how long to go on. How long did the ego have to be flattered, the image of self restored? How soon, in other words, could she tell him that there was a job going in a photography studio in town, a very down-market photography job for the great Gerry Moore, but she knew the man who ran it needed an assistant? Did she dare yet tell Gerry, suggest it to him, say that it would be a good idea for a year or two and he could build up his contacts after work? No, it must be too soon, otherwise why would she feel sick at the stomach even thinking about it?

That September they went to a wedding. They didn't know the people well and in fact they were rather surprised at the invitation. When they got there and discovered that they were among four hundred people it became clear that the net had been spread fairly wide. It was a lavish do and there was no effort spared to see that the guests had a good time.

'Isn't it marvellous to give two kids a send off like this — they'll remember it all their life,' Gerry had said. Something about the way he spoke made Emma look up sharply from her plate of smoked salmon. She stared at his glass. He was drinking champagne. She felt the blood go out of her face.

'It's only a little champagne for a wedding,' he said. 'Please. Please, Emma, don't give me a lecture, don't start to tell me it's the beginning of the end.'

'Gerry,' she gasped at him.

'Look, it's a wedding. I don't know people, I'm not relaxed, I'm not able to talk to them. Just three or four glasses and that's it. It's all *right*, tomorrow it's back to the everyday business of drying out.'

'I beg you . . .' she said. He had held his glass out to a passing waiter.

'What do you beg me?' His voice had turned hard and the edge of it, the cutting edge, had a sneer as well. 'What could you possibly beg from me, you who have everything?'

His voice was loud now and people were beginning to look at them. Emma felt the kind of dread and panic that she used to know as a child when she was at the carnival. She hated the carnival each year — the bumpers, the chairoplane and the ghost train. Most of all she hated the helter-skelter, and this is what it felt like now. Fast and furious and not knowing what lay ahead.

'Could we go home, do you think?' she asked faintly.

'It's only beginning,' he said.

'Please, Gerry, I'll give you anything.'

'Will you give me champagne, and fun and a bit of a laugh? No, you'll give me a lecture and a flood of tears and then if I'm very good a piece of shepherd's pie.'

'No.'

'What, no shepherd's pie? Oh, that settles it, I'll have to stay here.'

She whispered, 'But the whole life, the plans . . . the plans. Gerry, you've been so good, God Almighty, five months and not a drop. If you were going to have a drink, why here, why at this place, why not with friends?'

'I haven't any friends,' he said.

'Neither have I,' she said seriously. 'I was thinking that not long ago.'

'So.' He kissed her on the cheek. 'I'll go and find us some.'

He was sick three times during the night, retching and heaving into the handbasin in their room. Next morning she brought him a pot of tea and a packet of aspirins, half a grapefruit and the *Irish Times*. He took them all weakly. There was a picture of the wedding they had been at, of the young couple. They looked smiling and happy. Emma sat down on the bed and began to pour tea.

'Hey, it's after nine, aren't you going to work?' he asked.

'Not today. I'm taking the day off.'

'Won't they fire you? Recession and all that?'

'I don't think so. Not for one day.'

'That's the problem hiring married women, isn't it, they have to stay at home and look after their babies?'

'Gerry.'

'You told them you'd no babies, but still here you are staying at home looking after one.'

'Stop it, have your tea . . .'

His shoulders were shaking. His head was in his hands. 'Oh God, I'm sorry, poor poor Emma, I'm sorry. I'm so ashamed.'

'Stop now, drink your tea.'

'What did I do?'

'We won't talk about it now while you feel so rotten. Come on.'

'I must know.'

'No worse than before, you know.'

'What?'

'Oh, it's hard to describe, general carry-on, a bit of singing. A bit of telling them that you had had the cure and you could cope with drink now, a servant not a master . . .'

'Jesus.'

They were silent, both of them.

'Go to work, Emma, please.'

'No. It's all right, I tell you.'

'Why are you staying at home?'

'To look after you,' she said simply.

'To do sentry duty,' he said sadly.

'No, of course not. It's your decision, you know that well. I can't be a gaoler. I don't want to be.'

He took her hand. 'I'm very very sorry.'

'It doesn't matter.'

'It does. I just want you to get inside my head. Everything was so drab and hard and relentless. Same old thing. Dear Johnny, I don't know whether you remember my work. Dear Freddie. Dear Everybody . . .'

'Shush, stop.'

'No thanks, I'll have a Perrier water, no, thanks, I don't drink, no, seriously, I'd prefer a soft drink, nothing anywhere, nothing, nothing. Do you blame me for trying to colour it up a bit, just once, with somebody else's champagne? Do you? Do you?'

'No, I don't. I didn't realise it was so grey for you. Is it all the time?'

'All the bloody time, all day, every day.'

She went downstairs then and sat in the kitchen. She sat at the kitchen table and decided that she would leave him. Not now, of course, not today, not even this year. She would wait until Helen's fourteenth birthday perhaps, in June. Paul would be sixteen, nearly seventeen then. They would be well able to decide for themselves what to do. She made herself a cup of instant coffee and stirred it thoughtfully. The trouble about most people leaving home is that they do it on impulse. She wouldn't do that. She'd give herself plenty of time and do it right. She would find a job first, a good job. It was a pity about RTE, but it was too close, too near, in every sense. She could rise there and get on if she had only herself to think of. But no, of course not, she had to get away. Maybe London, or some other part of Dublin anyway, not on her own doorstep. It would cause too much excitement.

She heard him upstairs brushing his teeth. She knew that he would go out for a drink this morning. There was no way she could play sentry. Suppose he said he wanted to go out and buy something; she could offer to get it for him, but he would think up a job that he could only do himself.

There were maybe another thirty-five or forty years to go. She couldn't spend them with her heart all tied up in a ball like a clenched fist. She could not spend those years half-waking, half-sleeping in an armchair, wondering how they would bring him in. And even more frightening was sitting watching and waiting in case he broke out, the watching and waiting of the last five months. She would be blamed of course . . . selfish, heartless, no sense of her duty. Could you believe that anyone would do it? Emma believed that quite a lot of people could do it, and would if the occasion presented itself, or if the situation was as bad at home as hers was.

She heard Gerry come downstairs.

'I brought down the tray,' he said like a child expecting to be praised.

'Oh, that's grand, thanks.' She took it from him. He hadn't touched the grapefruit, nor the tea.

'Look, I'm fine. Why don't you go into work? Seriously, Emma, you'd only be half an hour late.'

'Well, I might, if you're sure . . .'

'No, I'm in great shape now,' he said.

'What are you going to do this morning, follow up some of those letters?'

'Yes, yes.' He was impatient.

'I might go in.' She stood up. His face was pure relief.

'Do. You'd feel better. I know you and your funny ways.'

'Listen before I go. There's a job going in Paddy's business, only an assistant at the moment, but if you were interested he said that he'd be delighted for you to come in, for a year or two, say, until you got yourself straight.' She looked at him hopefully.

He looked back restlessly. He didn't know that so much of his future and hers rested on the reply he gave.

'An assistant? A dogsbody to Paddy, Paddy of all people. Jesus, he must be mad to suggest it. He only suggested it so that he could crow. I wouldn't touch it with a barge pole.'

'Right. I just thought you should know.'

'Oh, I'm not saying a word against you, it's that eejit Paddy.'

'Well, take it easy.'

'You're very good to me, not giving out, not telling me what an utter fool I made of myself, of both of us.'

'There's no point.'

'I'll make it up to you. Listen, I have to go into town for a couple of things this morning, is there anything you . . .?'

She shook her head wordlessly and went to the garage to take out her bicycle. She wheeled it to the gate and looked back and waved. It didn't matter that people would blame her. They blamed her already. A man doesn't drink like that unless there's something very wrong with his marriage. In a way her leaving would give Gerry more dignity. People would say that the poor divil must have had a lot to put up with over the years.